The Art of Black Mirror Scrying

Rosemary Ellen Guiley

Visionary Living, Inc. New Milford, Connecticut

The Art of Black Mirror Scrying
By Rosemary Ellen Guiley
Copyright by Visionary Living, Inc., 2014
New Milford, Connecticut
www.visionaryliving.com
Cover design by Raúl daSilva

ISBN: 978-0-9860778-0-7

Contents

Introduction

Every day we look into mirrors to check our appearance, and see how others see us. Some of us know that mirrors have another, more mysterious nature—they have a long history of being able to penetrate the veil between worlds, and see into the land of the dead and the realms of spirits.

In fact, any reflective or shiny surface—metal, crystal, stone, a bowl of water, a still pond—has the same potential to pierce the veil. Instead of seeing our own face or the things in the world around us, we can see the dead, the astral plane, and the afterlife.

The power of the mirror to call forth the dead and spirits gives it high status as a necromantic tool. Necromancy is the summoning of the dead for the purpose of prophecy, that is, the revelation of things that are hidden. The ancient Greeks developed various ways of bringing forth the dead, including the use of mirror-like surfaces in special chambers or places called the *nekuomanteion*, or place of necromancy, Latinized today as "necromanteum." Another term that has been popularized is "psychomanteum," a term coined by Dr. Raymond Moody, one of the pioneers in near-death experience (NDE) research, to describe a meeting place with the spirits. (He also coined the term near-death experience.) Moody originally conceived of the psychomanteum as a tool for processing grief for the dead, but its uses have expanded into otherworldly journeying and contact with the dead and spirits for many purposes. The mirror of choice is the black mirror, for it enables a deeper and more profound altered state of consciousness.

I have experimented with both silver and black mirrors throughout my career in the paranormal. I have used them as tools for developing the intuition, for scrying (gazing) into the past and the future, and for contacting the dead and spirits. In 1994 I had my first experience with Moody, utilizing his private psychomanteum, and I became even more convinced of the power of the mirror. I describe my experience later on in this book.

I created my own psychomanteum and introduced others to the process of black mirror gazing. In 2008, I took training as a psychomanteum facilitator from Moody. I have continued my use of black mirrors, including the making of them. I do not use the mirror as a therapy tool, but as a gateway for altered states journeying. I prefer the term "necromanteum," which reflects the original meaning of a place for contacting the dead. The ancients traveled to remote, special areas believed to be portals to the underworld; these were the places of the dead. Today, the dedicated black mirror is the place, whether it is permanently installed or is small and portable.

The journey begins in the mind, and from there we can transport ourselves anywhere. The black mirror opens up amazing vistas. You may start with the intention to contact the dead, and find yourself looking into the future, or having an encounter with angels and other beings, or even encountering other life forms, such as those we call extraterrestrial. The mirror delivers what you need to see. Sometimes the mirror will not reveal a visual experience, but will facilitate profound insights.

Mirror gazing initiates a process that continues to unfold, in the stimulation of significant and lucid dreams; in flashes of intuition and inspiration; and in synchronicity, the meaningful coincidences that lead to turning points in life. You might have a mirror session that seems to produce very little at the time, and then you will go on the same or following night to have a vivid dream full of great importance. Perhaps the dream would not have happened without the seeding from the mirror gazing. We seek, and the means by which answers are delivered happen in their own ways.

Mirror gazing is to be taken seriously. It is not casual entertainment or a game, but a tool for one's spiritual path. The mirror has a formidable power. At times what it shows can even be unsettling, but that is where growth and Truth can be found.

This book will give you a blueprint for working with black mirrors. It covers the history of scrying, especially for consulting the dead; the modern uses of black mirrors; guidelines for mirror sessions; practical applications for personal growth; and how to create your own black mirror.

I have included some experiences and testimonials from individuals who have taken my black mirror workshops. Due to personal sensitivities, most people do not want full details of their names and situations disclosed, and so I have used first names only.

—Rosemary Ellen Guiley

1

The Magic Mirror

Alicia came to one of my black mirror workshops looking for a doorway to the afterlife. She wanted to contact her grandmother, who had died when she was 10 years old. She was now in her early thirties. Memories of Nanna were distant, and she wanted to reconnect with an important figure in her heritage.

After being coached on how to use the mirror, Alicia sank into the black surface and invited her grandmother to come for a chat.

In a black mirror session, time gets lost. It seemed to Alicia that she sat for a long time with nothing but a sea of shiny black in front of her. Then the surface of the mirror began to move like liquid and change. Briefly, she wondered if she was imaging it, then remembered my instructions to go with the flow. A gray-white mist, like fog or light clouds, appeared in the mirror, and then suddenly Alicia had a clear vision of the face of Nanna, as she had looked when Alicia was young. Alicia was flood with a sense of well-being and emotions of love. Then the face dissolved and the mirror returned to black.

"I felt Nanna was telling me she was all right," Alicia said in our post mirror-gazing discussion. "I didn't hear her say it in so many words, but I felt it, and also that she loved me very much.I also had a feeling that she was watching over me from heaven."

Also in the workshop was a middle-aged man named Tim, who sought to make contact with his younger brother, Greg. A car accident had claimed Greg's life three years earlier.

"I didn't see anything in the mirror itself," Tim said later. "But suddenly I could see him before me. I couldn't tell whether he was standing off to the side of me in the room or he was in my head, but he looked so was sharp and clear, it was like he was really there with me. I could hear his voice, clear as a bell. He said, 'I'm okay, Timmy, don't worry about me.'

"I said—I answered in my mind—'I love you, Greg. We all miss you.' He said there was a plan for everything and that was why he had to leave when he did. Then he said he had to go, and he sort of dissolved."

Both Alicia and Tim, as well as others who reach out to the dead through black mirror scrying, wanted to know if their experiences were "real" and not fantasy. The experiences are indeed genuine, taking place in an extension of reality that bridges our daily world to other realms, including the afterlife. The bridge is the mirror. What the mirror evokes varies according to the person. Sometimes there are detailed sensory impressions of sight and sound, and other times experiences are conveyed in mental and emotional impressions. There is no right or wrong to the mirror – you get the experience that is meant to happen to you.

What is it about the black mirror that opens such a powerful doorway?

The art of scrying

Gazing into a mirror—or any reflective surface—is a method of divination called "scrying." The term "scrying" comes from an English word from the early sixteenth century, "descry," which means "to succeed in discerning" or "to make out dimly." The scryer—the person who scries—fixes his gaze upon a shiny surface until images appear, either in the surface of the tool, or in his mind.

Sometimes the images are static, sometimes they move, like a film or video, and sometimes sound accompanies the images.

Divination is both looking into the future and seeking knowledge of the unknown. Since ancient times, humans have sought knowledge of the future in order to prepare for it or even try to change it. Humans have also sought knowledge of the unknown in terms of identifying thieves, criminals and culprits, finding lost objects, finding treasure, and finding sources of water.

In earlier times, the task of divination traditionally was carried out by priestly castes and magically empowered people, who interpreted their visions for their clients, who were usually powerful people and heads of state. Literally hundreds of methods of divination have been employed over the centuries. The dominant forms of divination since antiquity have involved shiny and polished surfaces: water, crystals, glass, mirrors, swords, spear and arrow heads, fingernails, wax, hand palms smeared with soot and oil, and more. Both silvery and dark reflective surfaces have been used.

From the eighteenth and nineteenth centuries on, divination became democratized, moving out of the grip of the priestly castes into the mainstream. Anyone today can practice divination via psychic training and the use of divinatory aids and tools such as cards, runes, crystals, pendulums, sticks, and so on.

In modern times, scrying has taken on a broader context beyond looking into the future.

Scryers can remote view distant locations and people, .
into past events and past lives, open the door to the afterlife, .a.
have contact and experiences with spiritual beings such as angels.

The black mirror is not a new wrinkle in scrying. In fact, many
scryers throughout the ages have preferred a dark reflective surface. The art of black mirror scrying was "lost," however, until several decades ago, when Dr. Raymond Moody—who pioneered
research of near-death experiences—reinvented it for the therapeutic purpose of contacting the dead. There will be more on Dr.
Moody later.

Where and when did scrying mirrors and shiny surfaces originate? The practice is as old as our earliest recorded stories, myths
and works. Even before mirrors came into common use, people
have been fascinated by reflections in shiny surfaces such as pools
of water. Mirror-like and reflective surfaces have always had a mys-
tique and an allure, revealing secrets, drawing the viewer deep into
their depths. At some point in our ancient past, people realized
that gazing at a reflective surface brought forth powerful visions,
and provided a way for the gods and spirits to be seen and for the
future to be known. The first discoveries might have been acciden-
tal, but people soon perfected the art of scrying.

Along with mirrors, people used whatever reflective surfaces
were available to them, as mentioned: water, crystals and shiny
stones, arrowheads, glass, wax, fingernails, swords, knives, ink,

...s a bowl of water was enhanced as a scry-
...ement of a crystal, shiny stone, coin, or piece of
bottom.

In Genesis 44, Joseph, the son of Jacob, refers to a silver cup that can be used for divination. There is no description of Joseph actually using the cup himself, or whether the divination was done by gazing at the silver metal or by gazing upon water in the cup. Joseph was already known among the Egyptians as an expert interpreter of dreams, and perhaps he wanted to appear to have other skills as well. Whether he actually scried or not, he knew the power of it.

The development of handmade mirrors

The first known handmade mirrors were not silver, but were black mirrors. They were made out of polished obsidian, and they were used in the upper class and royal households in ancient Anatolia, which is now part of modern-day Turkey. Circular, hand-held black mirrors dating to about 6000 BC have been discovered in excavations of Neolithic female burials sites at Catal Huyuk.

Mirrors were in widespread use in the Mesopotamian cradle of civilization: Babylonia, Assyria, Sumeria and Akkadia, as well as in Persia, Arabia and Egypt. Metal mirrors made of copper and bronze have been found in ancient Near East burial sites dating to about 4000 BC. From then on, mirrors were made with innovations and decorations; some were fashioned of gold and silver. They had devotional purposes for gods and goddesses in addition to personal uses by humans.

The ancient Egyptians had human-made metal mirrors of copper and bronze, the earliest dating to the Archaic Period, 3200-2700 BC. Leather, cloth, reed and wicker covers were made to protect their surfaces. The mirrors have been found in the tombs of both men and women, along with other possessions that were deemed needed in the afterlife.

The ancient Chinese and Indians made mirrors out of bronze, and ancient peoples in Central and South America made them out of polished stone.

Greek and Roman scrying

The ancient Greeks made mirrors of copper and bronze, and also used bowls of water and liquid, a type of divination called lecanomancy. The Greeks believed the dead possessed great knowledge, especially about the future, and that they were required to tell the truth; there was no sugar-coating of messages to please expectations. The process of summoning the dead—necromancy—was no small undertaking, and was usually reserved for important matters involving future events, so that the best decisions could be made. Typically, these concerned wars and politics. The dead were also consulted for pressing personal matters, and to solve murders and crimes. People also summoned the dead to lay, or exorcise the ghosts of the dead who were bedeviling them. In such cases, they would summon the dead person believed to be causing the problem, hear their grievance, and strike a bargain to appease the dead person.

Necromancy was done with the help of an intermediary: an oracle, priest or priestess, and sometimes a sorcerer or witch. The premier oracles of the dead resided in remote, sacred locations where subterranean openings to the underworld existed.

The process of summoning the dead (katabasis) was often elaborate, requiring fasting, purification and descent into a cave or chamber where the individual could have contact via scrying with a reflective surface, visions had in altered states of consciousness, and dreams that were incubated, that is, directed to a purpose.

Oracular sites for the dead were dotted throughout the Mediterranean. None of them were called a "psychomanteum." The Greeks instead used several terms, including:

—*Nekuomanteion*, meaning "prophecy place of the dead"
—*Psuchagogion*, meaning "drawing place of ghosts"
—*Psuchomanteion*, meaning "prophecy place of ghosts"

The term *psuchopompeion* or "sending place of ghosts" was in use by the second century.

By the fifth century, there were terms closer to those in use today: *nekuor(i)on*, meaning "seeing place of the dead," with a variant nekromanteion. A modernized and Latinized variation of this is "*necromanteum*," or "place of divining the dead," the term I use to describe the process of contacting the dead by scrying with a black mirror.

The Romans absorbed many Greek practices and put their own twist on them. Around the first century AD, Romans invented mirrors made of blown glass, but mirrors did not spread into general use. They were primarily used for divination by official scryers called *specularii*, from the Latin term *specere* ("to look at"). Their mirror was called a speculum, a term still used today to describe any scrying tool.

Glass and silvered mirrors

Blown glass mirrors later spread throughout Europe and were used for centuries. In the fourteenth century, glass blowing techniques enabled convex mirrors to be produced, increasing their popularity. Glass is not a good reflector, however, and during the Renaissance techniques were developed to coat glass with tin and mercury.

A big mirror breakthrough came in 1835, when a German chemist named Justin von Liebig invented a process for applying a thin coat of silver to glass, giving us the kind of mirror that is indispensable today.

The silvered mirror became a source of mystery and folklore beliefs about the supernatural. It was held that the mirror reflected both the body and the soul of the gazer. It served as a gateway to the spirit world, and to the afterlife. Some of the superstitions about mirrors are recounted in the appendix at the end of the book.

The silvered mirror never became a dominant scrying tool, however. For scrying, the black mirror or surface remained supreme, along with other shiny surfaces that allowed the scryer to see visions and not images of themselves. In fact—whether the mirror is black or silvered—the best results were obtained when the gazer turned the mirror so that he could not see himself in it.

Far-seeing mirrors

Legends and folk tales are full of stories of mirrors that penetrate vast distances. The legendary ancient Persian king Jamshid, as well as his successors, used a shiny cup to see what was going on in the entire universe. The pharaohs of Egypt reputedly had a mirror in a high brass turret that revealed the activities of distant provinces. According to lore, Alexander the Great put a mirror atop the lighthouse at Alexandria in order to see approaching ships that were still several days away. The mirror, which was said to measure three feet nine inches in circumference, was, by some accounts, made of crystal, and in other account made of a special Chinese steel or alloy of several metals. The Colossus of Rhodes statue also was said to have a mirror around its neck for monitoring the movements of distant ships. The Mexican god Tezcatlipoca possessed a golden mirror for spying on the entire world, as did the Celtic wizard Merlin.

In more recent times, the German fairy tale of Snow White features a magic hand mirror that reveals to an insecure queen who is the fairest in all the land.

The far-seeing mirrors of folklore were the forerunners of the powers of clairvoyance and the more modern term for the same, remote viewing. In the folklore, the mirror itself possessed the power. Today we know that the mirror is a tool that enhances the user's own psychic ability.

Far-seeing today goes beyond the physical world into the spirit realms, and through time.

Mirror men and women

The early divination practices of the ancients evolved into systems of occultism, magic and alchemy in Europe. Mundane purposes of scrying, such as looking for things and divination of the future, were joined with esoteric arts: the pursuit of spiritual knowledge, and the science of perfection.

Alchemy, the process of transmutation from imperfection to perfection, gained popuarlity from the late Middle Ages into the

Renaissance. Alchemy had two levels. One level concerned the search for a method that would quickly transform base or impure metals such as lead into silver or gold. It was another way to look for treasure, and, for impoverished or greedy rulers, to try and instantly fill their coffers. By the fifteenth century, Europe teemed with alchemists pursuing their secret arts, and though claims were made of successful metal transmutation, the hard evidence remains elusive.

The second level of alchemy concerned the spiritual perfection of an individual, via esoteric, occult and magical practices. The goal was to greatly increase longevity, youthfulness and vitality, and even to strive for immortality. The famous Comte de St. Germain, a real historical person who was mysterious and influential, was said to have discovered such secrets.

Alchemy and occultism were facets of the science of the day. The Renaissance scientist was also schooled in philosophy and the esoteric and occult arts. Some delved more deeply into the latter areas than others, and experimented with rituals and tools to access the spirit realms.

Some examples follow.

Artephius

In the twelfth century, the esteemed but mysterious alchemist and Hermetic philosopher Artephius conceived of a method that became known as "the three vases of Arthephius" that combined three techniques: the magic mirror, hydromancy (divination by water) and oinomancy (divination by wine). According to the method, a wooden table was prepared that was pierced with holes to receive the rays of the sun and the moon (an early concept of magnetism, which was developed more in the eighteenth and nineteenth centuries). Three vases were placed on it: an earthenware vase containing oil of myrrh; a green earthenware vase containing wine; and a white earthenware vase containing water. Substitutions of copper and glass vases were sometimes made for the second and third vases, respectively. A lighted candle was placed by each vase. The diviner had three tools: a poplar wand half stripped of its bark; a knife; and a pumpkin root. According to an anonymous manuscript that described the process:

> [B]y the earthenware vase the past is known, by the copper vase the present, and by the glass vase the future. He [Artephius] arranges them in yet another fashion; that is to say, in place of the earthenware vase a silver vase full of wine is set, and the copper one is filled with oil, and the glass with water. Then you will see present things in the earthen vase, past things in the copper, and future things in the silver... All must be shielded from the sun; and the weather must be very calm, and must have been so far for at least three days. By day

you will work in sunny weather, and by night in the moon-light and by the light of the stars. The work must be done in a place far from any noise, and all must be in deep silence. The operator is to be garbed all in white, and his head and face covered with a piece of red silken stuff or fine linen, so that nothing may be visible but the eyes... In the water the shadow of the thing is seen, in the oil the appearance of the person, and in the wine the very thing itself; and there is the end of this invention.

Roger Bacon

Another important figure who employed magical mirrors was Roger Bacon, (1214-1292), the earliest alchemist in England, known as "Doctor Mirabilis" ("Wonderful Doctor"). Bacon was a philosopher, genius and scientist far ahead of his time, anticipating by centuries the inventions of airplanes, automobiles, powered ships and suspension bridges. He reconciled the Julian calendar, though the changes were not instituted until much later. His work influenced the development of gunpowder, spectacles, the tele-scope, and advancements in astronomy. His unusual gifts earned him persecution, however. His unorthodox ideas were criticized and even banned by powerful opponents.

Around 1247, Bacon read *The Secrets of Secrets*, a spurious work on the occult attributed to Aristotle, but written by an anonymous person or persons. The book stimulated his interest in medicine, astrology, alchemy and magic, and he began a search for a universal science that would integrate all things. He sought to demonstrate that natural forces could be employed to create what appeared to be magic that is, the marvelous inventions of future machines that he envisioned.

His interest in alchemy was philosophical, and he especially saw it as important to religion and salvation. Medicine combined with morality and alchemy could increase longevity by several centuries. Astrology explained the correspondences between the body, humors, elements, stars and planets. All this ultimately was significant to religion, for it could explain the composition of human bodies before the Fall of Adam and Eve, and also explain how the souls of the damned would be tortured in hell. In a commentary on *The Secrets of Secrets*, Bacon said that God wishes for humanity to be saved, and provides through revelation the knowledge by which salvation can be obtained. Christian morality is key to longevity and to the success of science.

Bacon said that a person who has purified his body by alchemy could create a magical mirror for prophecy and divination. He called this mirror Almuchefi, and said it had to be made under the proper astrological auspices.

Bacon reputedly made and used such a mirror. Several centuries later, however, his scrying was twisted by the witchcraft craze that swept Europe and England at the hands of the Inquisition. The demonologist Johann Weyer accused Bacon of practicing black magic and collaborating with demons.

Catherine de Medicis

The wife of King Henri II of France was an occult enthusiast who made no decision with consulting her advisers and, according to lore, her magical mirror. When Catherine de Medicis (1519-1589) wanted to know who would succeed her son on the throne, her mirror revealed all future kings from Henri IV to Louis XIII and Louis XIV. After that came Jesuits, upsetting the queen so much that she nearly broke the mirror.

The dazzling Cagliostro

Count Cagliostro (1743-1795) was a flamboyant occultist who built his fame in part on his skill at scrying. He amazed royalty and nobility throughout Europe.

Cagliostro was born Guiseppe Balsamo in Palermo, Italy to a poor Sicilian family. Whether or not he had early psychic ability is not known, but by the time he was in his early twenties, he was determined to make a fortune, and did so in the fortune-telling business. He studied all the esoteric philosophies and arts, took initiation into the Order of the Knights of Malta, and changed his name to Count Alessandro Calgliostro. Later, he joined the Freemasons in England.

Cagliostro and his exotic wife and occult partner, Lorenza Feliciani, practiced crystalgazing, healing by a laying on of hands, conjuring spirits, and predicting winning lottery numbers, all framed in colorful rituals. They held seances and conjured the dead, including the prophet Moses, according to lore. They sold magical and alchemical potions. Cagliostro was so accurate in his predictions that he acquired the moniker "The Divine Cagliostro."

Cagliostro may have had talents himself as a scryer, but he favored the use of children, usually boys, in his public performances, thus drawing upon ancient practices. He said the boys should be as pure as angels in order to see visions. In a typical performance, he set a bowl or carafe of water on a table, and had his child scryer kneel in front of it. After praying to God for success, Cagliostro asked the boy what he saw. Critics of Cagliostro contended that he coached his children scryers and led them with questions.

Not surprisingly, the medical community scrutinized his alleged cures (which were making him wealthy), and soon Cagliostro lost favor with physicians and also the Catholic Church. He and Lorenza were framed in a fraud case unrelated to healing, and were jailed and put on trial. Supposedly, Cagliostro gained their release by spinning an elaborate story about being raised in Medina, Arabia, by a man, Althotas, who taught him his occult knowledge. He said his wealth came from the Sharif of Mecca, who mysteriously set up generous open bank accounts for him wherever he went.

Once freed, the couple went to England. The press, however, exposed Cagliostro's real and humble personal story, and his glittering, exotic reputation was destroyed. Even fleeing to Rome to start over did not help. The two were arrested and tried by the Inquisition. Cagliostro was found guilty of impiety, heresy and crimes against the Church, and was sentenced to death on April 7, 1791. Lorenza was sentenced to life imprisonment in a convent in Rome, where she is believed to have died in 1794.

Pope Pius VI commuted Cagliostro's death sentence to life imprisonment. He was sent to San Leo, where he spent four years in solitary confinement in a subterranean cell. Shortly after being moved to a cell above ground, he died, allegedly of a stroke, on March 6, 1795. Rumors that he miraculously escaped and remained alive persisted for years in Europe, Russia and America.

After his death, his spirit was summoned through mediumship and scrying by various seers. Francis George Irwin (1828 -1892), a high-ranking Freemason in England, used a crystal in his scrying seances, and during 1872-73 had several conversations with Cagliostro. The "count" told Irwin his crystal was of little value because it had been charged with an "antagonistic principle."

There is no elaboration of what Cagliostro meant by "antagonistic principle," but we can presume that he was calling into question Irwin's intentions in scrying. Irwin was known to be zealous in his pursuit of knowledge. Did he consciously or unconsciously "program" the crystal to serve egotistical ends? Apparently the "antagonistic principle" was not enough to keep Cagliostro's spirit away, since he made additional visits and obligingly dictated ritual material. The episode does underscore the importance of bringing the clearest and purest of intentions to scrying, ground rules that still apply to black mirror scrying done today.

The visionary bridge

Scrying, as well as other forms of divination, have had critics and opponents throughout the ages.

The Bible is full of important visionary experiences that influenced the patriarchs and prophets, yet religion has opposed divination as a false and even "demonic" art. Apparently what was suitable for the patriarchs and prophets is not suitable for the masses, and probably for political reasons. If a person has direct access to the spiritual realms, the mediation of the church is not needed, and the church loses control. During the Inquisition, scrying was considered a heresy.

Science has taken a dim view of divination as well, consigning it to fantasy and wish fulfillment.

None of this opposition has halted people from having spontaneous and intentional visionary experiences that are interpreted as real events. Dream encounters with the dead have been recorded for millennia (see my work *Dream Messages from the Afterlife*) as have waking visions and visions in scrying surfaces. Mirror visions fall in between the visions of near-sleep, in the hypnagogic stage, and waking visions. They are not fantasy or "hallucinations," but an experience that takes place in an alternate reality. Plato referred to a *metaxu* or "between state." Dr. Raymond Moody terms the visionary realm the "Middle Realm."

Philosopher and theologian Henry Corbin coined the term *mundus imaginalis*, or "imaginal world," to describe the intermediary world between the sensory plane and the spirit plane. The "imaginal world" is not fantasy. It is real. As Corbin stated in a 1964 essay, imagination should not be equated with unreality, but is a way of accessing an immaterial reality.

He described the *mundus imaginalis* as "a world that is ontologically as real as the world of the senses and that of the intellect.

> This world requires its own faculty of perception, namely, imaginative power, a faculty with a cognitive function, a noetic value which is as real as that of sense perception or intellectual intuition. We must be careful not to confuse it with the imagination identified by so-called modern man with 'fantasy,' and which, according to him, is nothing but an outpour of 'imaginings.'"

In pursuing visionary experiences, we must have the perspective that they are true and meaningful. Visionary experiences cannot be proved or disproved according to the prevailing understanding of science, but they have their own validity in the bridge realm between ordinary reality and alternate reality. In lore, mirrors reveal truth. In our exploration of the spiritual realm, mirrors reveal a personal truth that illuminates our life journey.

2

John Dee and Nostradamus

Two of the most famous scryers in history were John Dee and Nostradamus, contemporaries in an age when alchemy, magic and occultism intertwined with science, medicine, and the affairs and politics of life. Dee (1527-1608/09), an Englishman, used scrying to converse with angels to birth a new spiritual order. Nostradamus (1503-1566), a Frenchman, is famous for his prophetic visions, which he couched in mysterious quatrains that have been reinterpreted throughout the centuries. Both served royalty with their scrying skills.

John Dee

Dee grew up in a landed gentry household with royal connections and privileges. His excellent schooling plus his dedication to the pursuit of knowledge led to his reputation as one of the most learned men of his times. Alchemist, mathematician, astronomer and astrologer, he was steeped in Neoplatonic, Hermetic and Kabblistic philosophies of the day. Drawn from an early age to the occult, he was nicknamed "sorcerer" by his classmates at Trinity College. He gained renown in England in Europe for his lectures and knowledge, and amassed the largest private library in England.

More than anything, Dee wanted to have the experiences described by the occultists he admired. He wanted to have astral projections and converse with angels and spirits. He wanted to see the unseen and the future. Like many of his contemporaries, he believed the end times were fast approaching, and he desired to play an important role in ushering in a new order. In fact, he considered himself the messenger of Judgment Day.

Dee's efforts to secure royal pensions and patronage by casting horoscopes and providing advice were mixed. At one point, he was accused of treason by black magic for casting a horoscope to predict the death of Queen Mary. The information had been requested by Mary's half-sister and rival, Elizabeth. He was jailed but found not guilty.

When Mary died in 1558 and Elizabeth ascended the throne, the new queen relied upon Dee for astrological advice and lessons in occultism. His prestige gained him many prominent clients, among them Catherine de Medicis.

In his later years Dee's fortunes declined, in large part due to his obsession with scrying and his involvement with Edward Kelly, a man of dubious reputation. Dee died in obscurity in 1608 or 1609—the exact date is uncertain—and was buried at Montlake church.

As early as 1569, Dee was attempting to contact the archangel Michael in order to acquire God's wisdom. He had no success, but intensified his efforts, burying himself in his arcane books, dressing like a wizard, and performing rituals. He called his efforts his "Mystical Experiments."

He decided he needed the help of a partner, someone who had more mediumistic ability, and went through a series of men, some of whom produced conversations with angels. The first took place in 1581. In 1582, Dee had his fateful introduction to Edward Kelly through a mutual acquaintance. Kelly's shady reputation was well-known and also obvious: he had had his ears cut off as punishment for forgery. Kelly put on a good show of having access to the spirit world, and promised that he could deliver what Dee wanted. Kelly produced angels in their first scrying session, and Dee, impressed, hired him.

Not long after that, Dee actually had his own clairvoyant experience, one of the few he was ever to have in his life. He saw the archangel Uriel in a dazzling light. Uriel gave him a large crystal, about the size of an egg, by which he could communicate with spirits. Then the archangel Michael appeared and affirmed that Dee was to use this crystal as his new "shewstone." Dee did as instructed. He had the crystal set in gold, and forbade anyone else to touch it.

Kelly's performance with the crystal amazed Dee. He reputedly saw and conversed with angels, describing them in great detail. He delivered long instructions from the angels on magical numbers and squares, the construction of a scrying table, and activities that the two men were to undertake. While Kelly talked, Dee took laborious notes. According to the angels, Dee was the messenger of a new era, and was to take dictation on a holy book that would change the world.

The four main archangels, Michael, Gabriel, Raphael and Uriel, were prominent communicators in the scrying, as were a host of angels whose names were not known before.

The angels spoke in their own language, which Kelly translated and Dee recorded. The men also used a crystal globe in addition to the egg-shaped crystal. Dee also had a scrying mirror made of black obsidian, set in silver and inscribed with the names of the four archangels; the mirror is on display at the British Museum in London.

One of the principal "new" angels who appeared in the shewstone was Galvah, a female angel whose name, in their unique angelic language, meant "Finis" in Latin, or "the end." Dee and Kelly also referred to her as "the Maiden."

In her first appearance, Galvah said she was far from home and was on a journey that would end in about six to seven weeks, which marked a deadline set by the angels for Dee to make a "perfect copy" of the holy book.

"I myself will be the finger to direct thee," she said. "The finger of God stretcheth over many mountains. His Spirit comforteth the weakness of many places. No sense is unfurnished where his light remaineth. For understand what I am, and it is a sufficient answer."

According to the visions of her seen by Kelly, Galvah cast out a light whenever she spoke, and her appearances were heralded by a light in the shewstone. Once Kelly described a beam of light shooting out of the shewstone, going through the angel's head and coming out her mouth. She departed in light or by drawing clouds around her and disappearing into invisibility.

Dee recorded long conversations with Galvah. Other angels made appearances in the shewstone, too, and dictated more material. If Dee was to usher in a new era, he picked a problematic partner for completing the task.

Kelly was hot tempered, and the men had a stormy relationship. Somehow they managed to work together for seven years—even in spite of Kelly's assertion at one point that the angels had instructed the men to swap wives. Dee reluctantly agreed, but his wife threw a fit. There is no record that the swap ever took place.

The relationship between Dee and Kelly unraveled after they traveled to Europe to try to raise money advising royalty and noblemen, many of whom were interested in alchemy as a way to make a quick fortune. Dee and Kelly could never produce the formula for making gold out of base metal, and they were cast out of various places on accusations of fraud.

In 1588 they split and Dee returned to England. Queen Elizabeth, still his supporter, gave him a job as warden of Christ's College in Manchester, a position he found to be dull and boring.

He managed to hang on after Elizabeth died and James VI of Scotland succeeded her as James I; the king was a passionate opponent of anything smacking of witchcraft.

Declining into poverty, Dee retired to Mortlake where he continued his efforts in scrying, trying different partners but never achieving the results he had with Kelly. Sadly, he burned most of his diaries in frustration. What remained of his writings were not found until the late nineteenth century among his surviving belongings. They have been republished.

The new religion Dee envisioned never materialized, but his scrying work with the angels did have a profound impact on the development of the Western magical tradition, especially his magical numbers and squares, and his "angelical" language, which are still used today in Enochian magic.

Dee is an example of someone who worked better with a partner than alone in the process of scrying, although his choice of Kelly was not in the best judgment. Could Dee have done the scrying himself? It is possible that he tried too hard and expected certain results. Successful scrying requires letting go of expectations as to how the information will be presented.

Nostradamus

Nostradamus was born to a prosperous Jewish family that converted to Catholicism. From an early age, he experienced visions. His studies included occultism, the Kabbalah, Neoplatonism and astrology, which was expected of the well-educated Renaissance man. He became a licensed physician, and his remarkable work among plague victims—he had an uncanny gift for knowing unusual remedies that would work—gained him fame.

Nostradamus was in his mid-thirties when the plague claimed his wife and two children. Grief-stricken, he abandoned his job and wandered around Europe. He went deeper into his occult studies, and his visions increased. He remarried and settled down, and sometime after 1550 he began recording his prophetic visions. He said they came to him by "the subtle spirit of fire," delivered in fragments and accompanied by a voice from limbo which he believed to be the "Divine Presence." He summoned the visions by scrying late every night alone in his study, gazing into a bowl of water set on a brass tripod. He began his sessions with a magic ritual attributed to the ancient oracles of Branchus. He touched the tripod with a wand then dipped the wand into the water and touched the tip to his robe. He recorded the things he saw and heard, often not understanding them.

At the time, the Inquisition was still in force in Europe, and Nostradamus feared being accused of sorcery. He phrased the prophecies in rhymed quatrains written in a mixture of Greek, French, Provencal and Latin. Some words were further disguised in anagrams. He arranged the quatrains in groups of hundreds, or "centuries," which were not in chronological order.

The first prophecies were published in 1555 as *Les Propheties de M. Michel Nostradamus*, and were an immediate success in aristocratic circles, gaining him the favor of Catherine de Medicis and cementing his reputation as a prophet. He published a second, larger edition of *Les Propheties* in 1558.

Nostradamus enjoyed fame and success until 1566, when is health declined due to gout and dropsy. He died during the night of July 1 that year, and was buried upright in a wall of the Church of the Cordeliers in Salon. In 1791, superstitious French soldiers opened his grave. His bones were reburied in the Church of St. Laurent, also in Salon.

Occultism enjoyed a revival and boom in the nineteenth century, and the work of Nostradamus was celebrated. He was credited with observations that mirrors made better scrying devices than crystals, and afforded a closer contact with the spirit world.

Over the course of his career, Nostradamus wrote thousands of prophecies, plus almanacs, calendars and other writings. Scholars have puzzled over his mysterious quatrains for centuries. Some seem clear, while others have been interpreted differently, with a retro-fitting of historical events onto the quatrains. Some historians have held that he reworked ancient end-of-the-world forecasts.

Many people believe that Nostradamus foresaw events that have happened far beyond his lifetime. He is credited with having foreseen are the Napoleonic wars; the history of British monarchs from Elizabeth I to Elizabeth II, including the abdication of Edward VIII; the American Revolutionary War and Civil War; the rise and fall of Hitler; the assassinations of Abraham Lincoln, John Kennedy and Robert Kennedy; and the rise of the Ayatollah Khomeini.

He also is credited with predicting air and space travel, including manned rockets to the moon; and submarines that would be used for war; and the development of the atomic bomb.

The quatrains have been interpreted as predicting three reigns of terror by three Antichrists. The first two have been identified by some as Napoleon and Hitler; the third remains open to interpretation, but the scenario is similar to the end times portrayed in the book of Revelation. New York City would be destroyed in a nuclear war that would take place from 1994-1999. This great war was to be presaged by famines, drought, earthquakes and volcanic eruptions. After 27 years, the Antichrist would be defeated and killed, followed by a 1,000-year golden age of peace. Such events did not happen, but when the terrorist attack on the World Trade Center towers in New York City occurred on September 11, 2001, Nostradamians, as some students of his work are called, rushed to find validation for the event in his quatrains.

Nostradmus's predictions continue to be the focus of both controversy and scholarly study. Believers say he indeed could see several centuries ahead, while skeptics say that his veiled language enables the quatrains to be fitted to many events.

From the perspective of scrying, Nostradamus was true to his art. He followed a procedure that worked well for him, and let the visions arise without judgment. He acknowledged he did not understand them all, and he did not attempt to alter them; he let them stand. In scrying, especially for prophecy, the meanings of information may not be apparent until a later time.

If Nostradamus had recorded his prophecies in clear, direct

terminology, we would have a much better understanding of the content and validity of what he saw, night after night, in the dark mirror-like water of his scrying bowl.

3

A Mysterious Force

In the development of European alchemy and science during the sixteenth through mid-nineteenth centuries, scientists explored the ancient theory that a cosmic magnetic energy or substance connected all things together, governed the workings of the universe and all life on Earth, and influenced health and illness. According to Galileo Galilei (1564-1642), the Earth's axis was magnetically connected to a central force in space that connected to all things.

Scientists probed the properties of this mysterious magnetic energy that they believed emanated from all celestial bodies, including the planets and the moon. We know now fields of magnetism do surround planetary and celestial bodies. The Earth's magnetic field provides the basis for navigating directions, and it protects the planet from the powerful solar wind streaming out from the sun, which would strip away our protective ozone layer.

From an occult perspective—our focus here—magnetism also plays a significant role. In occultism, there is a psychic aspect to magnetism. It is the force behind psychic powers such as clairvoyance and healing, radiating out from human beings through the hands and the eyes.

Today this force goes by other names, such as the universal life force, prana, chi and other names. This force can be directed for energy healing, and can maximize psychic activities such as scrying. If you have ever practiced your psychic or intuitive skills, or participated in energy healing such as Reiki, then you have experienced what once was called magnetism.

Wizard Anton Mesmer

While Cagliostro was making his name and fame as an alchemist and scryer, a contemporary was achieving a bigger and more lasting fame. The first European to harness the occult properties of magnetism in a significant way was Franz Anton Mesmer (1734-

1815), an Austrian physician and Freemason whose work led to the development of hypnotherapy. To many of his peers, Mesmer's healing seemed magical. His use of magnets and the power of suggestion demonstrated the ability of will and consciousness to affect physical health. Mesmer's life and work were filled with high drama. His use of cosmic forces in healing was absorbed into occult principals governing scrying, and so it is instructive to delve into his ideas.

Mesmer was intrigued with the works of the alchemical greats, among them Paracelsus, Jean Baptista van Helmont, Robert Fludd and other scientists, physicians and philosophers, who believed that the powers of magnetism could be manipulated. A century earlier, van Helmont, a Flemish chemist and physician, had stated, "Magnetism is in action everywhere; there is nothing new in it but the name..."

Mesmer agreed with these greats that the ancients had been right, and these cosmic principles could be harnessed. As his own theories developed, he also borrowed from the ideas of Richard Mead, an English physician who in 1704 published a treatise on the power of the sun and moon on the human body—again based on ancient ideas. Mesmer was convinced that magnetism was an invisible universal fluid, and he named it "animal magnetism." He said it was vital to health, and the levels of it in the human body were influenced by the planets.

Mesmer's early ideas about animal magnetism were published in 1766 in his doctoral thesis at the University of Vienna. No one paid much attention, and Mesmer established a conventional medical practice. The treatment of the day was bleeding patients to remove the "ill humors" in their blood, and opiates. Mesmer found this and other therapies increasingly unsatisfactory.

His ideas about magnetism caught the attention of Father Maximilian Hehl, a Jesuit priest, court astrologer to Empress Maria Theresa, and professor of astronomy at Vienna University. Hehl also believed in a planetary magnetism that influenced physical health. He used magnets made in the shape of body organs to correct magnetic imbalances that he said were responsible for illness.

Hehl gave some magnets to Mesmer, who began placing magnets on his patients to ease or end their pain. He had spectacular healings. Mesmer concluded that his own body was a magnet, for he noticed that, when bleeding a patient, the flow of blood increased when he approached the patient and decreased when he moved away. The force of animal magnetism seemed to be transferrable from one person to another. A healer had excess animal magnetism and could transfer some of that to someone who was deficient in it, he said. The transfer could be accomplished through hand passes, a laying on of hands, and touching the patient with iron rods or wands.

Mesmer's breakthrough case was a 27-year-old woman named Franzl Oesterline, who suffered from "a convulsive malady, the symptoms of which were toothaches, earaches, vomiting, fainting, delirium and severe mood swings of anger. Mesmer used a magnet to ostensibly interrupt gravitational tides and drain away the fluids responsible for Oesterline's condition. The magnet enabled him, as the healer, to transmit his own good animal magnetism to the patient, which he accomplished with long and slow hand passes.

Mesmer published more on his theory of animal magnetism in 1775. The following assertions are in his words (note his references to the magnifying power of mirrors):

1. There exists a reciprocal influence between the heavenly bodies, the earth, and all living beings.

2. A fluid which is spread everywhere, and which is so expanded that it permits of no vacuum, of a delicacy which can be compared to nothing besides itself, and which, through its nature, is enabled to receive movement, to spread and to participate in it, is the medium of this influence.

3. This reciprocal activity is subject to the operation of mechanical laws, which until now were quite unknown.

4. From this activity spring alternating operations, which may be compared to ebb and flow.

5. This ebb and flow are more or less general, more or less complex, according to the nature of the origin which has called them forth.

6. Through this active principle, which is far more universal than any other in nature, originates a relative activity between the heavenly bodies, the earth, and its component parts.

7. It immediately sets in movement—since it directly enters into the substance of the nerve—the properties of matter and of organized bodies, and the alternative operations of these active existences.

8. In human bodies are discovered properties which correspond with those of the magnet. Also various opposite poles may be distinguished, which can be imparted, changed, disturbed, and strengthened.

9. The property of the animal body, which renders it susceptible to the influence of the heavenly bodies, and to the reciprocal operation of those bodies which surround it, verified by the magnet, has induced me to term this property Animal Magnetism.

10. The power and operation thus designated as Animal Magnetism can be communicated to animate and inanimate bodies; both, however, are more or less susceptible.

11. This power and operation can be increased and propagated through the instrumentality of these bodies.

12. Through experience it is observed that an efflux of matter occurs, the volatility of which enables it to penetrate all bodies without perceptibly losing any of its activity.

13. Its operation extends into the distance without the assistance of an intermediate body.

14. It can be increased and thrown back again by means of a mirror, as well as by light.

15. It can be communicated, increased, and spread by means of sound.

16. This magnetic power can be accumulated, increased, and spread.

17. I have observed that animated bodies are not all equally fitted to receive this magnetic power. There are also bodies, although comparatively few, which possess such opposite qualities that their presence destroys the operation of this magnetism in other bodies.

18. This opposing power permeates equally all bodies; it can also in the same manner be communicated, accumulated, and propagated; it streams back from the surface of mirrors, and can be

spread by means of sound. This is not alone occasioned by a deprivation of power, but is caused by an opposing and positive power.

19. The natural and artificial magnet is equally, with other bodies, susceptible to animal magnetism, without, in either case, its operation upon iron or upon the needle suffering the slightest change.

20. This system will place in a clearer light the nature of fire, and of light, as well as the doctrine of attraction, of ebb and flow, of the magnet, and of electricity.

21. It will demonstrate that the magnet and artificial electricity, with regard to sicknesses, possess simply qualities possessed in common with other active forces afforded by nature; and that if any useful operation springs from their instrumentality, we have to thank animal magnetism for it.

22. From instances deduced from my firmly established and thoroughly proved rules, it will be easily perceived that this principle can immediately cure diseases of the nerves.

23. Through its assistance the physician receives much light regarding the application of medicaments, whereby he can improve their operation, call forth more beneficial crises, and conduct them in such wise as to become master of them.

24. Through communication of my method, I shall, in unfolding a new doctrine of disease, prove the universal use of this active principle.

25. Through this knowledge the physician will be enabled to judge of the origin, the progress, and the nature even of the most intricate diseases. He will be enabled to prevent the increase of disease, and bring about the cure without exposing his patient to dangerous effects or painful consequences, whatever be the age, sex, or temperament of the patient.

26. Women, during pregnancy and in childbirth receive advantage there from.

27. The doctrine will, at length, place the physician in such a position that he will be able to judge the degrees of health possessed by any man, and be able to protect him from the disease to which he may be exposed. The art of healing will by this means attain to its greatest height of perfection.

The public reacted enthusiastically to Mesmer's ideas and promises of spectacular healing, and lined up as patients. True to his word, he produced amazing results, inspiring other to imitate his techniques.

Throughout the latter part of the eighteenth century and for part of the nineteenth century, the term "animal magnetism" referred almost exclusively to Mesmer's method of healing, which consisted of a laying on of hands, staring fixedly into the eyes of the patient, and making slow passes in front of the patient's face with hands or a wand. Patients who touched the wand experienced a tingling sensation and rush of energy.

Healers who modeled themselves after Mesmer were called "magnetists" and "mesmerists." In addition to curing ailments, magnetists could put their patients into a magnetized sleep (a state of hypnosis) which made operations painless.

The magnetized sleep produced certain interesting side effects, including clairvoyance, telepathy, mediumistic ability, hallucinations, suggestibility and catalepsy, a deep trance in which the body does not respond to stimuli and the muscles become rigid. Some "somnambules," as the hypnotized were called, could function as mediums and allow spirits to speak through them. Mesmer had little interest in studying any of these intriguing side effects, but occultists became quite interested in their applications for magical, mediumistic and psychic work.

As Mesmer's popularity rose, his medical colleagues who did not leap on his bandwagon became increasingly disapproving, perhaps in part out of jealousy. Criticisms arose of his techniques and the soundness of his theories. He fell out of favor with his patron Hehl and the Viennese medical profession, but patients still flocked to him.

The rejection of his colleagues greatly distressed Mesmer, who thought the truth of his ideas was proved by his results. Yet, he reexamined his work repeatedly, coming to the same conclusion every time, that he was right and the rest of his colleagues could not see the light. He expressed bitterness some of his writings:

> This system, which led me to the discovery of animal magnetism, was not the fruits of a single day. By degrees, even as the hours of my life accumulated, were gathered together in my soul the observations which led to it.
>
> The coldness with which my earliest promulgated ideas were met filled me with astonishment as great as though I had never foreseen such coldness. The learned (and physicians especially) laughed over my system, but quite out of place, however, for although unsupported by experiment it must have appeared fully as reasonable as the greater portion of their systems, on which they bestow the grand name of principles.
>
> This unfavorable reception induced me again to examine my ideas, however, of losing through this, they gained a higher degree of manifestation, and in truth everything convinced me that in science, besides the principles already accepted, there must still be others, either neglected or not observed.

In 1778, Mesmer moved to Paris where he expected better reception in the flourishing culture of alchemy, science and occultism. He set up a fashionable hospital that was more like a seance parlor than a medical facility, similar to the scrying rooms we create today for mirror work. The rooms were lit with low light, perfumed with incense, and decorated with mirrors, crystal objects, beautiful paintings and handsome clocks. Mesmer conducted himself more like a wizard than a physician, sweeping into his salon in a purple robe and brandishing an iron wand.

While a chamber orchestra played soft music composed by Mozart, which helped induce meditative and trance states, Mesmer and his assistants moved among the patients, waving hands and wands, stroking the patients and magnetizing them. Many phenomenal cures were accomplished, made all the more astounding by the hysterics and convulsions of his patients as they were cured. Rich and poor alike descended upon the clinic. Mesmer entertained well, hosting coffee socials and carrying on lively conversations with his clients. He was quite the celebrity.

So many patients came to his clinic that Mesmer had to treat them en masse. He created a device call the *baquet*, a round wooden bathtub which he filled with "magnetized water" and iron filings. Up to 30 iron rods protruded from the lid of the tub, which were placed on patients on whatever part of the body required healing, one rod to a patient. The patients were tied to each other with moistened rope, forming a magnetic chain. Patients called the tub Mesmer's "magic bath."

To his dismay, Mesmer began having the same problems with medical authorities in France that he had experienced in Austria.

He had the support of King Louis XVI, but even the king bowed to intense pressure from the Medical Academy to investigate Mesmer for fraud. In 1784, two Royal Commissions (one of which included Benjamin Franklin) conducted double-blind tests and concluded that results were the products of fantasy and touch, not the cosmic fluid described by Mesmer. In addition, Mesmer was set up by an enemy posing as phony patient who exposed him. The Academy moved to expel all practitioners of animal magnetism from their practices.

Another blow to Mesmer's fortunes came in 1784 when one of the most prestigious occultists of the day, Antoine Court De Gebelin, known for his work on the Tarot, died while sitting at a *baquet*. Court de Gebelin had been an enthusiastic supporter of Mesmer after the Austrian healed a serious leg infection in 1783. In 1784, Court de Gebelin had a relapse of the condition and sought more treatment, which led to his fatal day. It is doubtful that his death was actually caused by his treatment, but Mesmer's enemies seized upon it as proof that mesmerism was a dangerous practice.

Despite the setbacks, the public remained loyal and continued to patronize Mesmer. He managed to maintain his clinic until 1789, when the French Revolution forced him to flee the country. In Vienna, he was arrested on charges of being a spy for the French, and spent two months in jail. Upon his release, Mesmer returned to Lake Constance, where he died in 1815.

During Mesmer's life, occultism and magic were in vogue,

including methods of divination and performances of psychic powers and feats. Spiritualism emerged in the mid-nineteenth century. Many of the occult handbooks written during the nineteenth and early twentieth centuries discussed magnetism as an important force. The methods of Eastern and Oriental occultism, including scrying, were interpreted through magnetism as well.

Somnambules were widely regarded as pipelines of truth to the spirit world.

The Od

Among those who carried on research along the lines of Mesmer was Karl von Reichenbach (1788-1869), a German chemist and metallurgist, who used the term "Od" to describe an invisible, subtle universal energy comprised of magnetism, heat and electricity. The Od emanates from all living things, including crystals, and streams from the eyes. The term "Od" comes from the name of the Norse god Odin; Reichenbach considered Mesmer's term "animal magnetism" to be inadequate. Others following Reichenbach added to the name, calling it Odic force and Odyle.

Reichenbach sought to isolate this mysterious occult force. He conducted scientific experiments with psychics and mediums, and found that the Od could saturate matter and remain in it for periods of time. His work was validated by the society for Psychical Research in London. Nonetheless, he was rejected by the scientific establishment.

Astral light

"Astral light" is another term for magnetic fluid, animal magnetism and Od, with more complex dimensions that shed additional light on the workings of mirror scrying. The astral light has electric, magnetic and radioactive properties. The term "astral light" was put forward by the French occultist Eliphas Levi (1810-1875) in the nineteenth century to describe:

> ...an agent which is natural and divine, material and spiritual, a universal plastic mediator, a common receptacle of the vibrations of motion and the images of form, a fluid and a force, which may be called in some way the Imagination of Nature... The existence of this force is the great Arcanum of practical Magic.

The astral light is bound up in the faculty of imagination, which is crucial to the success of scrying. Levi said that the images of things and persons, even persons who have passed on, are preserved in the astral light and can be evoked, such as through scrying.

Israel Regardie (1907-1985), another leading occultist who served as the personal secretary of Aleister Crowley, elaborated further on the astral light:

Vibrating at another rate of motion than does the gross substance of the physical world, and thus existing on a higher plane, the Astral Light contains the builder's plan or model, so to speak, projected downwards by the Ideation or Imagination of the Father; the plan on which the external world is constructed, and within whose essence lies latent the potentiality of all growth and development.

Regardie said that every thought is impressed upon the astral light, which corresponds to the Akashic Records, the records of all things. All acts, thoughts and emotions of all forms, become impressed upon it for eternity. In mirror scrying, it is possible to access this repository to obtain information about past lives, the present, and even the future, for in esoteric philosophy, everything happens in an ever-present Now. It is only our sense of linear time that creates past, present and future.

Madame Helena P. Blavatsky (1831-1891), a founder of the Theosophical Society, which integrated Eastern occultism with Western practices, associated the astral light with the *Anima Mundi*, or World Soul, in her work *Isis Unveiled*:

The Astral Light or anima mundi, is dual or bi-sexual. The male part of it is purely divine and spiritual, it is the *Wisdom*; while the female portion (the spiritus of the Nazarenes) is tainted in one sense, with matter, is indeed matter, and therefore is evil already. It is the life-principle of every living creature, and furnishes the astral soul, the fluidic *perispirit* to men, animals, fowls of the air, and everything living.

It is important to have an awareness and appreciation of these concepts and forces, and to realize how deeply integrated we are into the whole of all creation. Your sense of connection will enhance your skill with the mirror.

4

Magnetism, Scrying
and Summoning the Dead

 The ideas of Reichenbach, Mesmer and others were absorbed into occultism. Scyers could summon animal magnetism or Od by gazing intently into their scrying surface, and could charge their tools with the force by making slow hand passes over it.

 William Britten, a Boston Spiritualist and husband of Emma Hardinge Britten, an English Spiritualist and clairvoyant, described the principle of magnetism in scrying in his writings in the late nineteenth century. Emma had been drawn into a London occult group that practiced using magnetism. The Brittens studied Eastern techniques as well. William wrote that one of the most effective ways to develop psychically "results from gazing intently on mirrors, crystals, precious stones, shining bodies, or pure fluids. The magnetic rays which are reflected back into the eye from these objects pierce the brain, and charge it with Astral light, whilst the fixidity of the action induces that self-magnetization which is the first step in somnambulism, trance, and ecstasy." He also stated, "Endless are the practices by which the ancients sought to obtain that divine direction which they prized, far above all earthly counsel or human judgment. They cultivated the art of crystal seeing, gazing into mirrors and still water to obtain visions."

Britten was impressed with a Bengali fakir (a Muslim Sufi ascetic and adept) by the name of Ali Achmet who had great scrying powers with mirrors. Other scryers employed boys and poured ink, walnut or fungus juice into their hands to "biologize" them for visions, but Ali Achmet kept a magical mirror in his apartment that revealed spirit faces, distant scenes, and of living persons residing in foreign countries.

Louis-Alphonse Cahagnet

One of the most enthusiastic adherents of magnetism was Louis-Alphonse Cahagnet, (1805–1885), who used it to create at least one kind of magical mirror. A Parisian cabinet maker by profession, Cahagnet saw demonstrations of magnetism in 1845 and was so impressed that he changed his profession. He became a magnetist, writing about the wonders of magnetism and of Spiritualism. Cahagnet used as one of his arguments the fact that he was a simple, uneducated man who found undeniable truth—a position that did not win him any favors with the scientific community.

Nonetheless, Cahagnet magnetized away, doing some healing but also spirit communications. Certain somnambules could enter a state of "ecstatic sleep," he said, a threshold to the spirit world. They could deliver messages from dead family members, find lost and stolen objects, and converse with famous historical figures.

One of the deceased historical figures that Cahagnet desired to interview was Emmanuel Swedenborg (1688–1772), a Swedish mystic who was an exceptional clairvoyant, and who taught himself how to enter deep trances in order to explore the spirit realms. Cahagnet was impressed with Swedenborg's work, but disagreed with some of it and wanted some clarifications.

Cahagnet's favorite somnambule was a young woman named Adele Maginot, who had a predisposition for mediumship from an early age. The two had a powerful rapport, and Cahagnet conducted dozens of seances with her, in which she diagnosed illnesses and made contact with the dead.

In several long seances, Cahagnet summoned Swedenborg, who appeared visibly to several people. He questioned the Swedish mystic at length, including his advice on talismans and magical mirrors. Neither of the latter two topics appeared in any of Swedenborg's voluminous writings, and there was no historical evidence that he ever used them; rather, he used advanced breathing techniques to enter into trance. Nor did Swedenborg work with a medium. Nonetheless, Swedenborg's spirit waxed on with advice on both topics, giving Cahagnet instructions for making a magical mirror. The spirit of Swedenborg asserted that he had owned and used such a mirror himself.

In his writings, Cahagnet revealed the formula:

> I promised not to reserve to myself anything I had learned from spirits. I will keep my word by giving the secret of the magic mirror, revealed to me by the Spirit of Swedenborg, who himself, possessed one, and of which I have already spoken. I made two in the way recommended to me, one of which I presented to my friend M. Renard, who after several experiments, gave a favorable report of it; mine was equally good. This is how we should go to work:
>
> Procure a piece of glass as fine as possible, cut it the required size, place it over a slow fire, at the same time dissolving some very fine black lead in a small quantity of pure oil to give it the consistence of a liquid pomade, which may easily be spread over the glass when well diluted. The glass being hot, incline it on both sides, in order that the mixture may spread of itself all over alike; then, the glass being placed on something quite straight and tight, let the mixture dry without disturbing it; in a

few days it will become as hard as pewter, presenting a very fine dark polish; put your glass in a frame, and after well wiping its surface, hang it up on a wall, as you would a looking-glass, but always in a false light. Place the person who desires to see a spirit, or a scene before this mirror, station yourself behind him, fixing your eyes steadily on the hinder part of the brain, and summon the spirit in a loud voice in the name of God, in a manner imposing to the individual looking in the mirror.

Even if the advice did not come from Swedenborg, the magical mirror and technique proved effective, and occultists later on even adopted the method of standing behind someone and projecting energy in order to manifest visions in a mirror.

As for the true identity of the spirit, validating the accuracy of scrying is of ongoing concern. More on the topic will be discussed later in the book. It is possible that Cahagnet and Maginot, in their zeal to contact Swedenborg, projected things onto the scientist that fit Cahagnet's agenda. As previously noted, no magical mirror ever surfaced in Swedenborg's surviving effects. Scryers must ever guard against making assumptions, or seeing what they want to see.

Cahagnet described other kinds of scrying mirrors, among them:

— The Theurgic Mirror, a bottle of clear water scried by a

child, who would receive answers in the form of pictures from the archangel Gabriel.

— The Mirror of the Sorcerers, commonly used in the countryside by seers and healers, which consisted of any kind of mirror or bowl or pail of water. After reciting a spell, the scryer saw visions in the water.

— The Mirror of Cagliostro, a bottle of clear water placed on a piece of furniture in front of a child. The scryer placed a hand on the child and asked questions; the child looked into the water to see answers in allegorical pictures.

— The Mirror of du Polet, a piece of tin with cardboard glued to one side and black cloth to the other. The scryer gazed into the black side.

— The Magnetic Mirror, a crystal globe filled with magnetized water.

— The Galvanic Mirror, two discs, one concave and made of copper and the other convex and made of zinc, both magnetized nine times in nine days. The scryer looked into the center of the concave disc.

— Cabalistic Mirrors, consisting of seven globes representing the seven planets. Each globes was made of the metal of the planet, and was consulted on the day ruled by that planet.

Eliphas Levi summons the dead

Some of the most dramatic mirror scrying work during the occult revival was done by Eliphas Levi, one of the great occultists in the nineteenth century. Levi, a flamboyant man, has often been called "the last of the magi." He is said to have coined the term "occult" itself as well as "astral light." He summoned the dead in an elaborate ritual using mirrors, an experience that changed him for life.

Eliphas Levi was the name he adopted during the evolution of his occult work. He was born Alphonse Louis Constant in Paris. His father was a poor shoemaker and had no means to provide for his son's education, so he was schooled at a local Catholic parish at the church of St. Sulpice. He freely spoke his mind on what he thought about Catholic doctrines, and soon was expelled.

Levi plunged into a study of the occult after the breakup of his seven-year marriage; his unhappy wife left him. He taught the Kabbalah, magic, the Tarot and alchemy, and quickly became famous throughout Europe. He became absorbed in the writings of Swedish mystic Emanuel Swedenborg. He was the first to draw a connection between the Kabbalah and the Tarot, aligning the 22 Major Arcana cards to the 22 paths of the Tree of Life.

During this time, Constant called himself Abbe Constant and dressed in clerical garb, though it is doubtful that he was ever ordained a priest. In the mid-1850s, he took the Hebrew equivalent of his name, Eliphas Levi, and wrote under the name Magus Eliphas Levi. His best-known work is *Transcendental Magic*, published in 1860, which presents his own system of magic, based in part on the *Greater Key of Solomon*. Other significant works by Levi are *The History of Magic*, *The Mysteries of the Qabalah*, *The Great Secret* and *The Book of Splendours*.

His works were translated into English, and had a great influence upon the key members of the Hermetic Order of the Golden Dawn, the greatest esoteric/magical lodge of the revival.

In the spring of 1854, Levi traveled to London for a change of pace and setting. He had letters of introduction to "persons of eminence." He quickly discovered that they had no serious interest in occultism, but wanted only to see him perform feats for their entertainment. He withdrew into private study of Kabbalism.

One day he returned to his hotel room and found an intriguing note waiting for him. It was a card torn in half with a half of a symbol on it—a partial seal of Solomon. A brief message told Levi to go to Westminster Abbey the following day at 3 PM, and the second half of the card would be given to him.

Levi complied, and on the morrow he was met by a footman and taken to a carriage. Inside was an elderly woman dressed in black and wearing a thick black veil. She handed Levi the other half of the torn card. They conversed, and Levi learned that she was an adept who had achieved a high, but not highest grade. She commended him for not bending to requests to show off his occult powers. If he promised not to divulge her name or residence, she would show him magical materials and a fully equipped magical cabinet. Levi agreed.

He went with her in her apartment, where they talked and Levi viewed her rare magical books and a cabinet equipped for ritual. The woman revealed her purpose for contacting Levi: she wanted him to evoke the spirit of Apollonius of Tyana, an adept who lived in the Roman Empire around the first century, who was reputedly quite skilled in clairvoyance, remote viewing and the magical arts. She had a question she wished to ask the spirit. Levi agreed to do it, and added a question for himself. The woman invited another person to participate, but this person withdrew at nearly the last minute.

Levi underwent elaborate preparations for the necromantic ritual for 21 days. He ate no meat for two weeks and fasted for a week. While fasting, he meditated upon Apollonius. In *Transcendental Magic* (1865), Levi described what happened:

> The cabinet prepared for the evocation was situated in a turret; it contained four concave mirrors, and a species of altar having a white marble top, encircled by a chain of magnetized iron. The sign of the pentagram... was carved and gilded on the white marble surface; it was drawn also in various colors upon a new

white lambskin stretched beneath the altar. In the middle of the marble table there was a small copper chafing-dish, containing charcoal of alder and laurel wood; another chafing-dish was set before me on a tripod. I was clothed in a white garment, very similar to the vestments of our catholic priests, but longer and wider, and I wore upon my head a crown of vervain leaves, intertwined with a golden chain. I held a new sword in one hand, and in the other I kindled two fires with the required and prepared substances, and I began reading the evocations of the Ritual in a voice at first low, but rising by degrees. [Reputedly these evocations went on for 12 hours.]

The smoke spread, the flame caused the objects upon which it fell to waver, then it went out, the smoke still floating white and slow about the marble altar; I seemed to feel a kind of quaking of the earth, my ears tingled, my heart beat quickly.

I heaped more twigs and perfumes on the chafing-dishes, and as the flame again burst up, I beheld distinctly, before the altar, the figure of a man of more than normal size, which dissolved and vanished away. I recommenced the evocations, and placed myself within a circle which I had drawn previously between the tripod and the altar.

There upon the mirror which was behind the altar seemed to brighten in its depth, a wan form was outlined therein, which increased, and seemed to approach by degrees. Three times, and with closed eyes, I invoked Apollonius. When I again looked forth there was a man in front of me, wrapped from head to foot in a species of shroud, which seemed more grey than white; he was lean, melancholy and beardless, and did not altogether correspond to my preconceived notion of Apollonius. I experienced an abnormally cold sensation, and when I endeavored to question the phantom I could not articulate a syllable. I therefore placed my hand upon the sign of the pentagram, and pointed the sword at the figure, commanding it mentally to obey and not alarm me, in virtue of the said sign. The form thereupon became vague, and suddenly disappeared. I directed it to return, and presently felt, as it were, a breath close by me, something touched my hand which was holding the sword, and the arm became immediately benumbed as far as the elbow. I divined that the sword displeased the spirit, and I therefore placed its point downwards, close by me, within the circle. The human figure reappeared immediately, but I experienced such an intense weakness in all my limbs, and a swooning sensation came so quickly over me, that I made two steps to sit down, whereupon I fell into a profound lethargy, accompanied by dreams, of which I had only a confused recollection when I came again to myself.

For several subsequent days my arm remained benumbed and painful. The apparition did not speak to me, but it seemed that the questions I had designed to ask answered themselves in my mind. To that of the lady an anterior voice replied Death! It was concerning a man of whom she desired information. As for myself, I sought to know whether reconciliation and forgiveness were possible between two persons who occupied my thoughts, and the same inexorable echo within me also answered Dead!

Levi was profoundly affected by this experience:

> The consequence... on myself was something inexplicable. I was no longer the same man; something of another world had passed into me; I was no longer either sad or cheerful, but I felt a singular attraction towards death...

Levi spent a great deal of time analyzing the experience. He did not know if he really evoked Apollonius, but could not deny the apparition, the touch, the answers or any of the other phenomena that occurred.

Levi repeated the experiment two more times, allowing for a break of several days between the two. The differences in the results were not sufficient to warrant description, he said, but the net result of the additional evocations were "the revelation of two Kabbalistic secrets which might change, in a short space of time, the foundations and laws of society at large, if they came to be known generally." He did not say what those two secrets were.

According to Levi, two things are necessary to acquire magical power: "to disengage the will from all servitude, and to exercise it in control." That is, we should not allow our will to be enslaved in any way, and we should exercise it with skill and rightful purpose. These principals are vital in successful psychic work. Practitioners cannot be enslaved to people, ideas, doctrines, institutions and so on, or they will be hobbled in the search for Truth. Mirror scrying is undertaken in the spirit of Truth.

5

The Psychomanteum

The occult revival faded in the early twentieth century, and when it renewed in the 1960s it took different forms. Scrying was a "lost art." Dr. Raymond Moody renewed the black mirror as a spiritual tool and updated its applications to modern needs.

Moody first became interested in mirror-gazing in 1986 during a visit to the home of his friend, parapsychologist William Roll. Moody asked about a crystal ball that Roll kept on a table in his living room. He was intrigued with Roll's explanation of the history and purposes of crystal gazing, chiefly seeing the future and conjuring spirits, but he took no action on the interest. Evidently Moody was supposed to act, for about a year later, he received a synchronistic nudge from the universe. He was browsing in a bookstore when a book fell off a shelf and landed at his feet. Its title was *Crystal Gazing* by Theodore Besterman, a classic work still considered to be one of the best surveys of the history of scrying with shiny surfaces.

This time Moody paid attention to the message. He began a study and first-hand investigation into ancient oracular practices of consulting the dead, and folklore about mirrors and shiny surfaces as doorways to other dimensions. His interest was further stimulated by research trips to Greece to investigate the oracles of the dead.

Moody immediately saw applications of this ancient practice for modern people, especially those in grief. How many times have therapists, counselors and ministers heard the grieving wish they had a chance for one last conversation with a beloved dead? More than anything—more than information, prophecy, estates and so on—the grieving want closure with the dead, a last chance to say, "I love you" or "I forgive you." What could be more powerful than an actual meeting with the dead, an evocation of their face and voice so real as to seem living again? The marriage of mirrors and a special sanctuary, combined with the rituals of therapeutic processing, could bring the dead alive again. Moody took the ancient oracular rite and transformed it into the psychomanteum, or the Theater of the Mind.

The psychomanteum is born

Moody began experimenting with mirror-gazing on his own, and then with others. His eventual ritual chamber was not a cave or subterranean labyrinth, but first his entire house and then a closet in his home. He covered the walls, floor and ceiling of the closet with black carpet, and set a large black mirror against one wall. An easy chair with the legs cut off was positioned so that he could see into the mirror without seeing his own, or any other, reflection. In dim light from a low-watt bulb lamp, Moody gazed into the mirror and asked to connect with his deceased maternal grandmother.

He tried not to have expectations. How would his grandmother appear? As an image in his mind, or as an image in the mirror? Old or young? Happy or sad? Would she look like a photograph or video, or like a ghost? Would she speak? He had read the descriptions of swirling gray clouds that form in crystal balls and mirrors that materialize into images of places and faces.

After long periods of concentration, nothing happened at all. Moody chalked it up to a failure. Two weeks later, he was sitting in a room when a woman walked in—it was an apparition of his deceased *paternal* grandmother, with whom he had not gotten along. She appeared youthful and transformed. He conducted a conversation with her concerning old times, especially his child-hood. After a period of what seemed like "timeless time," Moody reached a saturation point, said good-bye and exited the room. It was a healing experience, and he no longer felt a tension between himself and the memory of his paternal grandmother. He conclud-ed that even though he had desired to meet his maternal grand-mother, he was in need of closure with the other one. In his subse-quent experiments, Moody found that people tend to get the expe-rience they need rather than want, and that it is not unusual for results to be delayed and take place in other ways than mirror-gaz-ing. The mirror-gazing itself, however, is the pivotal experience that opens the door between realms.

Moody spent several years conducting research with mirror-gazing in his Theater of the Mind, and published his work in his book, *Reunions* (1993), co-authored with Paul Perry. Some of the cases were astonishing and compelling—stories of the dead who seemed so real they came out of the mirror, and of transports to eerie Twilight Zone-like dimensions where dramatic conversations and revelations took place. No matter how short the encounter, the impact on the living was powerful.

One woman described how her dead grandfather actually emerged from the mirror and held and hugged her as she cried. A man described how his dead mother appeared as being the age when she died, but looking healthier and more vigorous. She con-veyed telepathically that she was fine, and that it was good to see her son again. Then she vanished.

The response to *Reunions* was so great that Moody was hard-pressed to keep up with requests for appointments for psychomanteum experiences. Going through his psychomanteum was a half-day or all-day affair: preparation, time at the mirror, processing. Moody did many of these. Now he no longer conducts people through the experience himself, but prefers to teach others how to facilitate the process.

Some of the reaction was critical—skeptics found it hard to accept that the dead could reach out from a mirror and create the sensation of physical contact with the living. Do the dead really have the ability come out of the afterlife? The Greeks had no doubt that they did. Even today, people have intense lucid dreams in which they feel real physical contact with the dead.

Could not a mirror provide the right altered state of consciousness for a similar experience?

Initially, Moody thought that the visions in the mirror were hypnagogic imagery—the kinds of things we "see" in our mind's eye as we slip into sleep or drift into a reverie. But further research led him to conclude that the mirror literally takes us into what he called the "Middle Realm," another dimension where the living and the dead can meet. It is neither the ordinary world nor the afterlife, but perhaps is akin to the "between state" (*metaxu*) that Plato described as the land of dreams, where one can meet the gods and spirits. Another term for it is astral plane.

The growing literature on after death communications—experiences of contact with the dead—feature physical contact experiences. Some take place in dreams and some in waking visions, in which the living distinctly feel the physical touch of someone who has died. We cannot discount these experiences as wishful thinking and imagination, but rather believe that a true window opens between worlds.

In quantum physics, every universe has at least 10 dimensions, with time making up an eleventh dimension. These dimensions exist one on top another, but are usually not perceived.

We co-exist alongside these dimensions, and sometimes, when conditions are right, we can see into these other worlds.

The afterlife is one of these dimensions, and it is both accessible and inaccessible at the same time. People who have encounters with the dead or who see glimpses of the afterlife, such as in a near-death experience, often describe the other world as being "a blink of an eye away."

That's a layman's way of describing one of these dimensions in quantum physics. The dead are right next to us all the time, so close, yet so far away.

Throughout history, we humans have developed tools and methods for getting past the barrier. Even with our best efforts, the openings are fleeting.

Images of the afterlife

On several occasions, I have asked the mirror to reveal images of the afterlife. I have been shown glimpses of a terrain that resembles places on Earth, but with more vibrant colors and exotic shapes that may be unknown life forms, such as different "vegetation." It is difficult to assess such images in terms of their objective reality. Are they "real" or are they constructs fashioned out of the subconscious and even the collective consciousness, influenced by our beliefs in the afterlife?

We don't have records of what the average visitor to the *nekromanteion* experienced. The pilgrims were forbidden to discuss what happened, and so it is unlikely that accounts were written down. In all likelihood, few visitors probably wanted information about the afterlife—they were more concerned with what the dead could say about their problems, decisions and future. The Greeks regarded the afterlife as a drab and colorless place. The shades had no bodies, so it was hard for the living to conceive how the dead could enjoy the afterlife, bereft of physical sensations and pleasures. In the few records we have, when the dead appeared they conformed to the expectations of the living: they were somber or even unhappy, cold, deprived, and in want of what the living possessed.

Over the centuries, our views of the afterlife have changed. In general, we regard it as a "better place." The righteous are rewarded with comfort and the wicked are punished with deprivation and torture. Since the days of Spiritualism in the nineteenth century, few channeled descriptions of the afterlife conform precisely to religious depictions of heaven and hell, but they do reflect our collective views. It is likely that when we first cross over, we are greeted with environments that reflect our beliefs, in order to ease the transition. After a period of adjustment, we are likely to move into different conditions, but still reflective of our expectations. The astral plane is fluid and pliable and responds to thought. At some point, we may evolve into environments that are presently hard for the living to comprehend.

So, it is not surprising that psychomanteum visions of the afterlife reflect our personal, cultural and collective thoughts on what we find after we die.

A similar influence may affect our visions of the dead. The Greeks had no pearly, idealized visions of the dead. Today, we spontaneously see the dead as healed, youthful and full of light and energy – visions of them at their prime. If we believe that the afterlife is a better and more idealized place where souls are restored and rewarded, these images make sense.

In the long run, we may not be able to determine what the afterlife is "really" like. It may be all things reflecting all beliefs. The black mirror delivers information and images that are important and real to the viewer.

Evaluating psychomanteum imagery

Researchers have debated whether or not psychomanteum images are the same as, or comparable to, hypnagogic and hypnopompic images, which are seen in the borderlands of consciousness between waking and sleep. (Hypnagogic images are seen as we fall asleep and hypnopompic images occur as we wake up.) They are usually jumbles of faces and other fleeting images, and also bits of sounds and voices.

Hypnagogic/hypnopompic imagery is not quite the same as mirror gazing imagery—anyone who is experienced in visioning work would distinguish them as well. Psychomanteum images are seen with the eyes open, while the twilight sleep images are seen with the eyes shut, more like dream imagery. The hypnagogic and hypnopompic images often seem random and without context or meaning, while psychomanteum images usually are meaningful to the session. The images that emerge during a psychomanteum session have their own objective reality, emanating from another dimensional realm. Whether you see them in your mind's eye or projected into the environment does not matter. The effects vary from person to person. Parapsychology researchers have found that hypnagogic/hypnopompic and psychomanteum states of consciousness are "psi conducive" for telepathy, clairvoyance and precognition. That certainly fits the ancients' experiences of successful divination and prophecy.

The psychomanteum experience varies for each person, of course, but it can be so vivid that for a brief time the dead seem to come alive again, and sometimes look and sound so real that they might literally step out of the mirror. A psychomanteum experience can allow a person to have a conversation with someone who has died. For the grieving, even a brief few words can bring about closure.

6

My Visit to the Psychomanteum

In 1994, I had the opportunity to go through Raymond Moody's psychomanteum. I traveled to his home in Alabama, where his Theater of the Mind was still set up in a walk-in closet. I was quite excited, not only to go through a psychomanteum experience, but to have my first with Raymond, the pioneer in the field.

My goal was to contact my father, who died in 1982. I had always felt close to him, and shortly after his death, I had a dream visit with him (which I relate in *Dreams Messages from the Afterlife*). I had read *Reunions*, and I hoped that the black mirror would enable me to have a new encounter with him.

The psychomanteum process took the better part of a day. After lunch with Raymond and his wife, Cheryl, Raymond and I took seats in his spacious, antique-filled living room. Raymond sat in his favorite chair, an overstuffed rocker covered in blue velvet. He rocked back and forth as we talked about the history of mirror-gazing and his ongoing research of oracles in Greece.

Raymond discussed his views of the black mirror as a tool that can further understanding of the near-death experience (NDE) and aid work done with the dying. Apparitions of the dead often appear during an NDE, and frequently, terminally ill people begin to see apparitions of the dead as their own death approaches. Perhaps mirror-gazing might alleviate the anxieties of the dying, and help NDErs integrate their experiences.

Into the psychomanteum

After this general discussion, Raymond took me upstairs to the third floor where the psychomanteum was located. We ascended a narrow, winding staircase covered with a cream and burgundy paisley carpet runner. The third floor had an attic look, like a secret place where one goes for refuge. Light was dim. There were books and old furnishings, an antique desk piled high with Raymond's writing journals, another overstuffed rocking chair covered in mauve velvet, an antique armchair with a high back and arms, and an enormous mauve hassock with carnival legs. The space felt comfortable, pleasant and secure.

Raymond settled in the rocking chair. I took the armchair facing him, and put my feet up on the hassock. He put a box of tissues on the armrest. I didn't expect to need them, as 12 years had passed since my father's death, and I considered myself long past the grieving. I just wanted to experience him again. Raymond, however, knew better, that talking about the dead often evokes strong emotions, no matter how many years have passed.

Raymond began a gentle inquiry into my relationship with my father: its high points and low points, favorite memories, painful moments, happy times, how we related to one another. As I talked, I looked at a photograph of Dad that was taken about a year before he died. It was the only thing I brought with me—the few of Dad's personal effects that I have saved over the years were packed away in storage boxes.

Much to my astonishment, reliving my relationship with Dad did bring on buckets of tears. I wondered, does grief ever truly end? Perhaps it doesn't—we just find ways to cope with it, to diminish it.

It seemed as though Raymond and I talked for a long time. Time is something that is suspended in the psychomanteum: there are no watches, no clocks, no calendars to remind you of where you are in linear space-time. The idea of the experience is to break the bounds of time and space in order to access other dimensions where time and space have no meaning.

When I was finished talking about Dad, Raymond ushered me in to the small chamber that was the psychomanteum itself. The floor, walls and ceiling were covered in black fabric and carpet. On one wall was an enormous, arched mirror in a gilt rococo frame. Facing it was a winged armchair with its legs removed, so that the body of the chair rested directly on the floor.

Behind the chair was a tiny Tiffany lamp with a dim bulb. The mirror was silvered, but the black chamber that was reflected in it made the surface appear black and bottomless.

I sank into the chair. From this vantage point, I could look into the mirror without seeing any reflection of myself, the chair or the lamp. Raymond removed the stained glass shade of the lamp. The low, indirect lighting illuminated the frame, but left the mirror surface itself a bottomless, inky pool.

Raymond gave me a blanket and extra cushions, and told me to relax. Stare into the depths of the mirror and don't try to force a vision, he advised. I would have the best chance of success if I could drift into a hypnagogic state without falling asleep. He said he would leave me in the psychomanteum about an hour to an hour–and–a–half, longer than a typical session of 30 to 45 minutes.

He closed the door. The edges of the room blurred in the semi–darkness. There was only me and the mirror.

I gazed into the mirror, going beyond the surface into its infinite depths. I thought about Dad and relaxed. Soon there was movement in the mirror. A smoky film arose, followed by dull gray clouds. I watched the images without being attached to them. As I continued gazing into the mirror, it seemed the light in the room shifted and dimmed. Suddenly it seemed quite dark, and the only thing visible was the gold frame of the mirror, which brightened to brilliant neon gold.

The mirror seemed to grow larger and come closer to me, as though it would swallow me. I wanted to be drawn into its depths, but there was a boundary that kept me back.

The clouds returned, and they coalesced into a shape—a being of light. It was human-like in shape, visible from the shoulders up. The head had shadowy suggestions of eyes, but no facial details. It seemed to be composed of glowing, golden-white light, surrounded by a halo penetrated by streaming rays of light that went off the boundaries of the mirror.

The image moved in the mirror so that I can see it from various angles.

I asked mentally, "What am I seeing? Is it an angel? Dad in a new form?"

Mentally, I received an impression that I was looking at a light body, a form beyond form.

The being of light stayed with me, alternately fading into the mirror and returning in brilliant glory.

After what seemed like 10 or 15 minutes, Raymond softly cracked open the door to the psychomanteum. The mirror lost its magical depths and returned to a black reflective surface. He asked how I was doing. An hour and 15 minutes had passed. It was hard for me to believe that so much time had gone by.

I left the chamber and joined Raymond to discuss my experience. I was somewhat disappointed not to experience Dad photographically as I remembered him, but I was excited about the light being. Raymond said that other visitors to the psychomanteum had similar experiences with visions of light or angelic beings. He said that I might have follow–up experiences in the days and weeks ahead that would illuminate this initial voyage.

We talked for a while longer, and then I departed. I spent much of the remainder of the evening integrating the experience, alternately thinking about it, and then letting it permeate my consciousness and work on its own while I occupied myself with something else.

A follow-up experience

The morning after my journey into the black mirror, I had another experience. I awakened in the early morning hours in my dark Alabama hotel room. Across the room and in front of the bed was a large silvered mirror. I gazed into it, mulling over my experience of the previous day, and allowing my mind to wander.

Suddenly I heard a voice in my mind. It told me that I had been shown a light body, which was the true body of the soul, a vibration of energy. This was the real essence of my father—and of all souls. The physical form we take in an incarnation exists eternally, and can be accessed, such as in mirror visions and in dreams. But the locus of the soul is a pattern of energy, and was shown to me in the form of a light being, something I could recognize.

I had had a meeting with Dad after all.

The ongoing journey

My journey into the mirror continued to have reverberations. Overall, it was a positive experience that expanded my thinking. I had long believed that the soul takes on a new form of light in the after-death world, but had not changed my own perception of the dead: I still thought of Dad as he was in his physical form. This state of being continues to exist in some reality, yet is not the sole vehicle for the soul essence. The experience also benefitted my creativity. I felt opened, with greater access to the unconscious, and to higher levels of energy as well.

I did have to cope with a tumult of emotions that resurfaced, having to do with my relationship with Dad, and with his death. The emotional side of the mirror journey is one reason why Raymond strongly recommends that people work with a partner or a therapist.

A few days after my journey, I talked with Dianne Arcangel, a therapist and counselor in Houston, whom Raymond trained in the psychomanteum process. Arcangel had her own psychomanteum, and a portable version as well.

Arcangel told me that encounters with light beings rather than apparitions of the dead are frequent in the psychomanteum. She agreed that the mirror shows us what we need to see.

The necromanteum is born

Prior to my psychomanteum experience, I had experimented with silvered and black mirrors as tools for psychic development. The psychomanteum was such a powerful experience that I decided to continue working with black mirrors for the purpose of contact and spiritual development.

In 2008, I had the opportunity for another hands-on experience with Raymond, a weekend workshop in psychomanteum facilitation training in Asheville, North Carolina, sponsored by Joshua P. Warren. While Raymond lectured and answered questions, each participant went off one by one to spend time in a psychomanteum set up in one of the hotel's rooms. In this setup, a background of white noise was added as an enhancement.

This time, the mirror—a small black mirror set up on a shelf—showed me a number of things. I had visions of past lives, and at one point, two alien beings emerged out of the mirror and came into the room. I was entirely comfortable the entire session, and at the end, the beings and the visions slipped back into the mirror.

As I stated in the introduction, I decided to call my own black mirror sessions and workshops the "necromanteum" to describe a place of contact with the dead, which is the purpose that most people pursue with this tool. The black mirror opens many doors beyond the afterlife.

7

Choosing, Preparing
and Caring For Your Mirror

New mirror, old mirror, handmade mirror... what should you get?

When I became interested in black mirror scrying, I found them hard to find commercially, even in metaphysical stores. Many of the ones I found were more art objects than functional psychic tools. For a time, I worked exclusively with a black mirror made by a friend, Marcus Leader. Then I decided to make my own. I still have the other mirror and use it in addition to my favorite.

As we've seen in earlier chapters, people have been quite inventive about scrying tools, using whatever shiny surface is handy. Remember, the tool is the enhancer to your ability, not the ability itself. I have experimented with many scrying methods, and the black mirror is one of my favorites.

Choosing a mirror

Most people buy a black mirror rather than make one. There are advantages to buying one already made. It's ready to go, and it has been imbued with the energy of the maker. If you acquire your mirror from someone in the psychic arts, that enhances the background energy of the mirror. You will put your own energy into as well.

My husband Joe and I began making mirrors to acquaint people with this powerful ancient art. We put a great deal of time and energy into selecting the components. During the actual making of the mirrors, we focus and invoke spiritual intention and energy into the process.

When the mirrors pass from our hands to yours, they have been made and blessed for enlightenment, truth and benefit.

When you buy a mirror, hold it and see how it feels from a psychic or gut intuition perspective. If it does not "light up" for you, so to speak, pass on it and try another one.

Mirror glass

A black mirror is glass that has been coated on the underside instead of silvered. Some mirrors are coated in flat black paint and others in glossy paint or enamel. Both flat and glossy paint afford a good reflectivity.

Any kind of glass can be transformed into a black mirror. Some people prefer convex glass, which they feel offers a better depth. Plain plate glass works equally well, in my opinion.

Frames

In earlier times, it was said that a black scrying mirror should be framed in silver, which has associations with the moon and psychic work. Actually, any kind of frame is suitable. I avoid frames that are busy or full of reflective decorations.

I believe a black mirror scrying tool should have a certain aesthetic. We look for interesting frames. Most of our frames are new, but we also find vintage frames that we feel are suitable for the purpose.

Size

Is there an optimum mirror size? I have scryed in huge black mirrors that filled up nearly an entire closet wall, and in little mirrors small enough to slip into my purse. People have scryed with fingernails and drops of ink held in the palm of the hand.

Personally, I have found that an 8 x 10-inch surface size is ideal. This size is easy to stand up on a table or shelf, and can be stored away when necessary. It is the size I prefer for my classes and workshops. Mirrors that are 5 x 7 and 4 x 6 inches in surface size work well, too. I have made round mirrors, square mirrors and rectangular mirrors of even other sizes.

Mirrors that are mounted on walls and in closets can be much larger. Keep your environment in mind. The larger the scrying surface, the more it will pick up background reflections that you will have to minimize or eliminate.

Preparing and caring for the mirror

Your black mirror is a sensitive tool and should be treated with care and respect. Newly acquired or made mirrors should be cleansed and consecrated before first use. Mirrors should also be cleansed after use and before storage. There are many methods for cleansing and consecration, from simple to elaborate. If you already follow a particular magical or spiritual path, you probably have a favorite ritual. I prefer simplicity. I have experimented with a variety of methods, and have found that the key element is in your intention. A simple procedure, done with the right mindfulness and intention, gets the job done.

Residual energies

Why do scrying mirrors need to be cleansed, especially if you haven't used a new one for the first time? All objects pick up residues of energy from the people who handle and own them, and from their environment. Psychics and seers throughout the ages have obtained information by handling objects and possessions, and getting impressions from them. Years, decades and perhaps even centuries after someone has owned an object, a psychic, by handling it, might be able to see the owners, see snippets of their lives and where they lived, and experience their emotions. For example, if a ring was owned by someone who led an unhappy and tragic life, a psychic might feel profound sadness upon handling it.

In the early nineteenth century, the process of obtaining information from objects was given a name: psychometry. The term "psychometry," from the Greek words psyche (the soul) and metron measure), was coined in 1840 by Joseph R. Buchanan, an American professor of physiology who saw psychometry as a means to measure the "soul" of objects. Buchanan conducted experiments in which students could identify drugs in vials simply by holding the vials.

Buchanan's work interested Professor William F. Denton, an English professor of geology, who conducted his own experiments in 1854 with his sister, Ann Denton Cridge. When Cridge placed wrapped geological specimens to her forehead, she experienced vivid mental images of their appearances. Denton recorded his experiments in a book, *The Soul of Things*. He defined psychometry as a "mysterious faculty which belongs to the soul and is not dependent upon the body for its exercise."

How does information become recorded in objects? No one knows, and science has no explanation. Some materials hold information better than others. Best are metals, followed by stones, crystals and glass, and then wood. Any material, however, can retain residues. If an object has been owned by more than one person, the impressions can become muddy or mixed. When I give readings, I ask the client for a personal item that I can hold, preferably metal, like a watch or jewelry, which has not been owned by anyone else. Even car and house keys work. Holding the objects magnifies other impressions I receive, and as well delivers additional ones.

A scrying mirror collects residual energy, too—the "animal magnetism" known in earlier times. When the mirror is new, it has a patina of energy from its creation (even in a manufacturing process) and handling. The patina that is spiritually imbued by hand making is good. When the mirror is used in scrying, it collects the energy of the scryer and of the scrying sessions that layer on top of any psychic charging it has received in its making. For maximum effectiveness, the mirror should be energetically fresh. When you use it over and over, it will collect a patina from you, which in psychic and magical practice is considered advantageous, for it makes the tool more effective as time goes on. But you don't want the stray residues of sessions collecting and clogging up the channels.

In psychic and magical work, a rule of thumb holds that you should not let others use your tools, whether a Tarot deck, pendulum, wand, mirror or other object. Having others participate in a scrying session, such as clients or observers, is fine, for they will not be linked to the mirror in the way you are linked. But don't lend out your mirror.

A single mirror can be dedicated to a group purpose, however. For example, I have worked with paranormal investigation groups who have a black mirror as one of their tools. Even in a group, it is still best to designate one or two persons to be the official scryers and handlers.

For the mirror workshops that I conduct, I have a special set of mirrors devoted to that purpose. The mirrors are given a cleansing after each workshop so that they will be fresh for the next workshop with another set of users. Prior to the start, I give them a tweak to clear any stagnant energy that might have accumulated in storage.

Cleansing

First gently clean your mirror with damp a cloth that has been dipped in warm water. You can also use glass cleaner—spray a cloth and apply. Clean only the front surface. Do not take the mirror apart and wipe the black underside, because you will damage the black coating. Do not put the mirror under running water for the same reason.

The frame can be cleaned according to its composition: silver, wood, composite, resin, metal, or other materials. While you are cleaning, also wash the mirror in positive thoughts: how beautiful it is, how much you will enjoy working with it, what a valuable tool it is, the mirror will always show Truth, and so forth. Imagine your energy streaming into the mirror.

Sage and incense smoke are excellent spiritual cleansers, and can be fanned over a mirror. Recite a favorite prayer for spiritual cleansing and protection.

You can also cleanse the mirror with white light. Visualize it bathed in white light that removes unwanted energetic residues and impurities. In the fashion of the magnetists, let white light stream from your eyes, too, for the body is a channel for the universal life force.

Salt is an excellent spiritual cleanser, but I do not recommend sprinkling a mirror with salt, because grains can lodge between the frame and the glass. Salty water may damage the frame. You can employ salt as an environmental cleanser when you scry, however.

Do not expose the mirror to intense sunlight as a way of cleansing it. Mirror scrying works on lunar principles that govern psychic, spiritual and intuitive forces, and is best done in dim light.

After you've cleansed the mirror, you may want to personalize it by adding symbols or decorations to the frame or the back. Keep the scrying surface free and open.

Consecrating and charging a mirror

You've now put a lot of your own energy into your mirror, but there is still more to do. Psychic work is spiritual work, and should always be conducted in pursuit of Truth, enlightenment, healing, assistance and benefit. This is your primary intention, and it should also be imbued, or charged, into the mirror. You must honestly feel and believe this in the depths of your heart and being.

The mirror should *never* be used for selfish purposes or manipulation. The best time to consecrate the mirror to the forces of Light and charge it for Truth is during the waxing moon or at the full moon, and in the evening hours. Some people also factor in astrological auspices.

Place the mirror in front of you and light two white candles, one on each side of the mirror. Envision yourself protected in a circle of white light, and offer a prayer for spiritual protection. Call upon the assistance of only those in other planes—spirits, guides, angels, the ancestral dead—who will work in Light and honor Truth.

Dedicate the mirror to the Light and Truth. With great force, imagine the vibrations and energy of Light and Truth streaming into you and the mirror. Imagine your own energy streaming into the mirror. Hold the mirror and continue to feel the stream of energy filling you and enveloping and penetrating the mirror.

Magnetize the mirror by making slow hand passes over it. Passes with the right hand will enhance the mirror's strength and power. Passes with the left hand will enhance its sensitivity.

The mirror will be fully charged when you feel the energy peak. It is now ready to use.

You do not need to rededicate or recharge it every time you use it. When you have finished a session, cleanse the mirror, such as with white light or incense. Wiping the mirror with the intention of cleansing is effective, too.

You can reconsecrate and recharge your mirror at any time, however, if you feel it needs it. If the mirror sits for a long time without use, you can give a goose of energy.

Storage

Some people keep their black mirrors out all the time, such as on altars, on walls, or on display.

Others prefer to store the mirror when not in use; this is what I do. The advantage of storage is that the mirror is away from the idle curiosity of others, who may wish to handle it, and also it is at less risk of damage from accidents. Make sure it is adequately protected from damage and exposure to temperature and humidity extremes.

If you do keep your mirror out, place it where the face will not be in direct sunlight.

8

Using Your Black Scrying Mirror

Your black scrying mirror is a powerful tool that can assist you in many ways. It can be used to contact the dead and spirits; see the afterlife and other realities; access and validate your intuition; help you make decisions; remote view the past, present and future; review your other lifetimes; incubate dreams; gain information from the Akashic Records, develop your psychic skills, and much more.

The mirror stimulates third-eye psychic attunement, and when you use it, you are working on the astral plane, which is a plane of existence that lies next to the physical realm. The astral plane has no natural landscape of its own, but is white and formless. It consists of astral matter, which is fluid. Duplicates of everything in the physical world exist on the astral plane, and pre-exist everything on the physical plane. The afterlife exists in the astral plane, as do the abodes of spirits and various beings. Navigating the astral plane is often like moving through a dreamscape. Do not expect the mirror to reflect ordinary reality, but a surreality which can seem dreamy and fantastical, but has its own validity.

Mirror results vary by individual, and include visions in the mirror; visions in the external environment; and mental visions and thought impressions. Black mirror gazing is likely to stimulate dream activity. Results may be immediate, and/or may occur in the days following a scrying session, especially with intuitive flashes, synchronicity, and inspired dreams.

For best results, approach a scrying session as you would any serious spiritual activity. Set aside time when you can be relaxed, centered, focused, and ready to work. Turn off the phones, let others in the household know that you are not to be disturbed. Mirror scrying can be done around the clock, but many people prefer the quiet and intensity of the nighttime hours.

Come to the mirror with a specific purpose, such as an answer to a question, or to see into another reality.

The scrying environment

A dedicated area

You may be fortunate enough to have a large closet or other space that you can dedicate solely to scrying. Most people, however, find a suitable place in their living quarters, usually a bedroom or study that affords privacy and can be shaded from direct light.

A dedicated scrying room can be customized with featureless dark walls, floor and ceiling, and controlled light sources. In living quarters, use the select a spot that you can use repeatedly for scrying sessions.

Wherever you elect to scry, you can place personal items that are important to your spiritual work, such as crystals and other stones, medallions, figurines, and so on. If you store the mirror after each use, you can keep those items handy in a small box. See the appendix on Portable Altars for more ideas.

Lighting

Always work in dim light, which fatigues the physical eyes and helps the psychic faculty to emerge. Use low-wattage bulbs or candlelight. You can intensify the effects by using 25-watt blue bulbs in your lamps. Red bulbs work, too, but blue light will fatigue the eyes much quicker. Stained glass lamps will soften the glow even more. If you work with your mirror propped up on a table, put a flameless tea light candle behind it. The light will cast a soft and dim aura around the mirror. Do not use a real candle, not even a tea light, because the open flame close to the mirror will pose a fire hazard.

Mirror positions

The mirror should be as blank as possible when you look into it. For most types of scrying, you especially do not want to see yourself in the mirror, or see any lights or lamps in the mirror. (One exception to seeing yourself is the exploration of past lives.)

If you use a table top, you can try either standing the mirror up or laying it flat. Laying it flat has an advantage of pointing up at the ceiling, which is usually featureless. If you prop it up on a table or hang it on the wall, position either the mirror or yourself to minimize reflections of other things in the room. If you scry in your living quarters, you may not be able to eliminate everything in the background, but minimize reflections as much as possible.

Experiment with positioning the mirror until you find what works best for you. If you hang it on a wall, place it at a height so that gazing into the center of it will be at about eye level.

How far away you sit from the mirror will depend on its size. You should be close enough so that the black field of it absorbs all your attention.

Your chair or seating should be comfortable and not a distraction. Sit no more than three feet away from the mirror. Some people feel it is important to align the mirror to compass directions; for example, sit so that you are facing north, or east, etc. North is the direction of Uriel, the archangel of Truth, and east is the direction of Gabriel, the archangel of revelation.

However, you can orient yourself according to your purpose, including west for Raphael's healing, or south for Michael's access to the dead. If ambient light or background reflections limit the placement of the mirror, you can mentally set your compass.

Sound

Some people like to play soft meditation music in the background while they are scrying. White noise, such as the sound of a fan running, water running, gentle static, and so on is conducive to altered states. You may prefer silence. Once again, experiment.

Elements of scrying sessions

Mirror work should be done when you feel rested, calm and centered. Eat lightly, for a large meal dulls your senses. I often like to have a gentle herbal tea prior to mirror work, and in my workshops I am sometimes able to offer a custom blend of soothing and relaxing ingredients such as chamomile, catnip and skullcap. While I drink the tea, I focus on what I expect to accomplish with the mirror. I do not advocate using psychotropic drugs, which can introduce wild card and overwhelming elements into psychic work.

Timing

Is there a best time of day or night? Opinions vary. One old crystal gazing guide I have states that the best times are sunrise, midday and sunset, and the hours between 10 PM and 2 AM should be avoided. However, I believe you should scry when the time is right for you. Ideally, that is when you are refreshed and in a good frame of mind, as noted.

The deep night hours are more conducive to spirit contact in powerful ways, and can be unsettling for some people. If working at night unsettles you, switch to daytime hours. Do not scry if you are fatigued, anxious, depressed or upset.

Starting the session

Seat yourself in front of the mirror. Offer a prayer for spiritual protection, and for the presence of your guides, who may include angels, gods and the ancestral dead. Some scryers cast a magic circle around them for protection; the circle is then ritually taken down at the end of the session.

Others are more informal. I work daily on spiritual connections via meditation, which builds up a natural protective environment. My own technique before mirror scrying is to connect with that protective presence around me, as I set my intention for the session.

Setting intention

Ask for Truth to be revealed for whatever purpose you have. For example, if you seek communication with a dead loved one, you might frame your request like this:

"I come to the mirror to speak with my father. I wish to tell him _____, and I would like to know _____."

If you are exploring a past life, you might phrase your purpose like this:

"I come to the mirror to see a past life that will help me understand _____ or help me heal _____. May truth be revealed, show me what I need to know."

To ask for guidance on problems, decisions and so on, you might phrase your purpose thusly:

"I come to the mirror to find answers to _____."

Whatever your purpose, make it clear and focused. Otherwise your session may be vague and unproductive.

Relaxation

Relax yourself physically and mentally. This can easily be accomplished by using the breath and a few visualizations. Focus on breathing in slowly and deeply, imaging the breath being carried by golden white light. It fills your body from the top of your head to the soles of your feet.

Breathe out slowly, imaging the breath-light flowing out through the soles of your feet into the earth. The breath-light penetrates every part and cell of your being to relax and center you. If distracting thoughts arise, just let go of them, as though they fall through a sieve. Even experienced meditators have intrusive thoughts. If stray thoughts pop up at any time during your session, gently let them go and refocus yourself in the mirror.

The mirror gaze

Gaze steadily into the mirror. Slightly unfocus the eyes. Imagine the mirror as a liquid black pool and allow yourself to enter it, even fall into its soft depth. The black mirror opens to a great void in which many things can be discovered.

Keep gazing steadily and easily into the mirror. If your attention drifts, return it to the mirror. Let go of distracting thoughts, but do pay attention to thoughts that pertain to your purpose.

Do not try to force results. Your gaze should always be relaxed and effortless in order for the psychic faculty to kick in.

Once you are deep into scrying, you should be in a light trance similar to the borderland between waking and sleeping, and you will lose sense of the passage of time. Scrying takes you into a time-less reality.

Mirror gazing has a window of productivity, and then fatigue sets in. Keep a timer with a gentle chime at hand to signal the end of a session. The most productive time lengths vary by individual, but generally 30-45 minutes is the optimum. Sessions that are too long lose their focus and can be quite tiring.

Initially, you may feel quite fatigued after only five to ten minutes. The more you practice, the easier it will be to have longer sessions.

As impressions and information develop, do not try to analyze them on the spot, and do not discard or ignore anything. You can spend plenty of time in analysis after the session is done.

A digital recorder is a handy aid for capturing all details. Describe what you see, hear, feel and sense, as impressions arise.

Closing the session

To close, return your full focus to the room and center yourself in your body, using deep breaths. Feel your breath flowing out through the soles of your feet, anchoring and grounding you to the earth. Give thanks for the session, and mentally close the door of the mirror.

Allow time to reflect on the session and take notes. Mirror gazing is like dreaming, and details may be easily forgotten.

9

Evaluating Scrying Results

Results with a black mirror vary considerably, depending upon how an individual receives and processes psychic information. Some people are highly visual, some are more attuned to sound. Some people are prolific dreamers and others rarely remember a dream.

Beginners may have a learning curve with few results at first. Don't worry—the mirror will do its job in the ways that are best for you. Do not expect high drama, and look for subtleties. You will get information but not necessarily in ways you expect. For example, the dead might not show visually in the mirror. Instead, you might get impressions about them, or mental messages from them. Some messages might be quite specific while others might be general, such as conveying a sense of their well-being.

The more you practice with a black mirror, the more adept you will become at navigating other realities. You will learn more about how your own psychic faculty works as well. Over time, you will notice that your intuition will function better and more prominently in all facets of daily life.

You must be open to how the mirror responds to you. Do not hold on to preconceived ideas that you should see dramatic images, or feel physically transported to another reality. Mirror scrying involves more subtleties than drama.

Common mirror phenomena

Any or all of these phenomena may occur:

- —Cloudiness in the mirror, including moving clouds
- —Pinpoints of light in the mirror
- —Images that flash in the mirror or remain steady
- —Images that move
- —Images that appear in the mind while the mirror remains blank
- —Mental voices and sounds
- —Symbols and images that have personal symbolic meaning

—Environmental sounds, such as voices that seem to manifest in the air around you

—Answers, information and "knowing" that seem to fall into your mind

—Little or nothing during the session, but intuitive flashes and breakthroughs later, and/or dreams that deliver what you are seeking

—Intense emotions

In some cases, the mirror will deliver something different than what you've asked to see. You get what you need, not necessarily what you want. Pay attention. Psychic tools have a way of taking us to the heart of something that needs to be addressed.

Psychic work can release intense emotions, including feelings that have been buried and forgotten. You may be surprised to be flooded with emotions during and after a session, such as unresolved grief, anger, or self-defeating beliefs. All of these may be the seeds of profound healing. Issues may arise that should be addressed in professional counseling.

Accuracy

You are likely to second guess your results until you gain confidence in your scrying. You will wonder if you made it up or projected your own desires. You will wonder about the accuracy.

You will then discover that your accuracy is far greater than you expected, perhaps even astonishing. Most people do not think of themselves as psychic, or give themselves credit for their natural ability. It's understandable—we aren't conditioned to think that way.

One of the primary rules of psychic work is to allow impressions to arise without judgment. What arises or appears first has validity. If you discard it because you think it "can't be," then you are likely to get nothing more, or you will force something that is not accurate.

Remember, psychic work delivers what you need, not necessarily what you want. With practice, you will gain trust in the process.

Assessing accuracy is sometimes difficult, depending on the type of scrying and the results. If you are seeking a message from the dead, you can examine it at face value. If you are divining the future, then you probably will have an opportunity to validate your accuracy. No medium, psychic or seer has ever had a 100 percent track record of accuracy, but many are quite good. Keep in mind that you are looking at probable outcomes of forces in motion, all of which can change to at least some degree. As mentioned before, the more you practice, the better your results. Astral work, which is where psychic work takes place, is quite fluid. You will learn to move along with the currents of energy.

If you are using the mirror for remote viewing (see the chapter on Mirror Experiments), you are likely to have opportunities to gauge your accuracy as well.

Answers in symbols

In some instances, the mirror will deliver answers and information that are direct and easy to understand. In other cases, results will be couched in symbols, feelings and perceptions that require interpretation. Many times, mirror work is like dream interpretation.

Do not discard impressions that on the surface seem to make no sense, or do not seem related to your inquiry. If you ask a question and get a symbol, ask yourself what the symbol means to you, and how it might shed light on your question. You might have to put it in the back of your mind and let it incubate for a while. A dream dictionary of symbols is a useful guide to helping you find meanings.

Your own lexicon

Over time you will learn your own "vocabulary" for knowing what certain phenomena mean. Clouds that move one way might signify yes and another way no. Clouds of different colors will carry different meanings. Pinpoints of light might indicate the opening of interdimensional doorway or the presence of certain beings. Phenomena are usually accompanied by intuitive information. It may be helpful to learn how others interpret their data, but one person's system may not apply to another. You will develop a unique relationship with spiritual forces.

When I was studying energy healing with Mietek and Margaret Wirkus, I would often ask if a symbol I got was the right symbol. Mietek's answer was, "What does it mean to *you*?"

Unsettling and disturbing experiences

It is not unusual to feel unsettled, even disturbed, by mirror work, especially in the beginning. Mirror gazing may seem mysterious and spooky. Many of us have been conditioned by film, television and novels to think that creepy things happen with mirrors.

It is true that mirrors—usually silvered mirrors—have a long paranormal history. They are a powerful tool for opening inter-dimensional doors, and I have seen them occasionally figure in problem hauntings. In such cases, there is usually a badly placed mirror in a home or building that already has troubling paranor-mal activity. Ideally, mirrors should not be placed at the foot or head of beds; nor should mirrors look into each other. A general rule of thumb is to not have mirrors placed anywhere in a bed-room so that you can see yourself in bed. However, keep in mind that people sleep peacefully with mirrors in their bedrooms all the time.

Your black mirror is a tool that has a dedicated purpose. Use it responsibly. Do not use it for reckless and open-ended spirit summoning, for thrill seeking, or under the influence of alcohol or drugs. Close the interdimensional door at the end of a session. Thank whoever has come into the mirror and announce that the door is closing between worlds, and they will remain in their world and you in yours. Recognize that there may be a big difference between being unsettled by the mirror and disturbed by the mirror. Psychic images, flashes and true but unexpected answers can be unsettling. They originate in nonordinary reality. Also, when we undertake psychic work, we have to be committed to dealing with difficult matters when they arise. If you are disturbed by the mirror and carry over fear and anxiety into daily life, then you should not use the mirror, at least until you ascertain why you are having those reactions.

If at any time during a gazing session you feel unsettled or disturbed, end it and close the door. Over time you will become more accustomed to the nature of psychic work. It is a good idea to school yourself as much as possible concerning alternate realities, psychic functions, and paranormal phenomena so they lose their "strangeness." You will discover that the real psychic world is vastly different from portrayals in film, and especially many of the so-called "reality" television shows that are filled with people running and screaming all the time.

It is important to be grounded and well-balanced in any type of paranormal and psychic work, including mirror work. If you bring anxieties and fears to the table, they will reflect back to you. Some people are not well-suited to this kind of work because of their temperament, so know yourself and your boundaries.

10

Enhancing Scrying Results

Black mirror gazing, like all psychic work and exploration, requires practice, dedication and patience. There are a variety of fun and interesting ways you can improve your performance.

Training exercises

If you are new to mirror work and to psychic work in general, you can tone up with training exercises that will help you develop your mirror perception. Sit in front of the mirror in dim light, relax, and gaze into the blackness. Imagine that you are able to see an image sharply and clearly in the mirror. For example, call to mind a circle in a bright color such as red. Imagine it materializing out of the depths of the blackness. Hold it in the mirror, then let it dissolve. Call up another image, such as a green triangle.

Simple geometric shapes work the best, in bright primary and secondary colors. This technique is similar to a psychic training format using geometric shapes on cards called Zener cards. You can expand into other images as well—houses, things in nature, even people you know. You can add sounds as well, letting them manifest internally.

Other images to train with are people you know and places that are familiar to you. When you visualize, call up as much detail as possible.

A variation used for the past century is this: Sit in front of the mirror and then look at something else in the room, such as a piece of furniture. Notice as many details as possible. Then look into the mirror and call the image into it. Progressively make the target images more complex. Next, close your eyes and visualize something in the room, then open your eyes and transpose the image to the mirror.

These exercises will loosen up the imagination, which plays a key role in psychic work. Using your imagination in scrying does not mean that you make something up. Imagination is by definition "the faculty or action of forming new ideas, or images or concepts of external objects not present to the senses." All psychics, seers and visionaries of all kinds, even corporate visionaries, have the ability to give their imagination free reign. They see or perceive the unseen, the unmanifest, and the possible.

Psychic and intuitive development

Learn how to use other psychic tools, such as dowsing rods and pendulums, Tarot cards, remote viewing, and runes. Classes, workshops and self-study guides are available everywhere. Courses for "intuition development" accomplish the same thing; they just use different terminology for those who are afraid of the word "psychic."

Dreamwork

Dreams speak in symbols, and so are quite similar to psychic impressions. As mentioned, scrying often affects dreaming, with answers and information coming via that medium. If you are not in the habit of paying attention to dreams, start a dream log. Instruct yourself at night to remember your dreams. Even if you have difficulty remembering dreams, small fragments may contain mother lodes of information.

Classes, workshops and self-study guides will help you learn your own dream landscape.

Meditation

A daily or regular practice of meditation improves all kinds of psychic and paranormal work. Meditation teaches you how to still and focus you mind and concentration. It strengthens your connection to the spiritual realms. It improves your natural protection against unwanted influences.

You don't need to meditate like a monk or a yogi, and there is no such thing as "not enough time." When something is important enough, people always find the time for it. A few minutes of meditation a day will produce wonderful results. You may not see them in an obvious way, but after a while, you will realize that you think differently and perceive things differently, and you have a core calmness you did not have before.

There are many meditation techniques. Years ago, I learned Zen techniques that I still use today. However, simply sitting in a comfortable chair, relaxing the body with the breath, and stilling the mind works for many busy people. When others tell me that they can't sit still, or they can't focus their thoughts for long, then I know they are not ready for this kind of work.

One way to still the mind and let go of distracting thoughts is to visualize a pearl. Whenever thoughts intrude, return to the pearl. Sometimes I use a form of active meditation to start my day. I sit quietly and set an intention, something I want to accomplish. I always end meditation with thanks for all the blessings that I have in life. Never take anything for granted.

Play and humor

Engaging in other creative outlets enhances psychic work because creativity works the imagination and intuition. Playfulness and humor help as well. Have some child-like fun!

Herbs

Earlier I mentioned that I often like to drink an herbal tea prior to scrying (and dream incubation). Herbs that relax are helpful, and I have found some that enhance the vividness of imagery. Teas that contain chamomile, lavender or a touch of skullcap are good. You don't want a sleep sedative tea, however, just a relaxing, soothing tea.

Years ago I discovered that catnip enhances dream imagery, an effect that I corroborated with other in the dreamwork community. Catnip for humans is not toxic. You can find commercial tea blends that have some or all of the ingredients I have mentioned. Or, you can go to a herbal apothecary and have a custom blend made, which is what I do for some of my workshops.

During the heyday of magnetism, it was held that teas and infusions of the herbs mugwort and chicory, taken during the waxing moon, were particularly useful for scrying because it was believed that these herbs were responsive to magnetic influence (they turn their leaves to the north). Today mugwort is used in many relaxation and sleep tea blends, and in folklore it is said to enhance dreams. Chicory can be found in many forms. When dried and ground, it is blended into coffee. Cultivated chicory includes radicchio and endive; you can add them to your salads and food.

May you have productive journeys!

11

Mirror Experiments

As you gain more familiarity with the mirror, you will be inspired to invent different techniques for working with it. Here are possibilities, all of which have been proven effective:

Mirror meditation

Combine mirror gazing with deep meditation. Set your intention, gaze into the mirror, and then close your eyes and withdraw into a meditative state. If you are a highly visual person, you may find that this lessens eye fatigue and enhances mental images.

Mirror meditation is particularly useful for certain kinds of journeying, such as into past lives or the Akashic Records, as discussed below.

Past-life scrying

You can get glimpses of past lives in the black mirror. Focus your purpose as much as possible. Rather than asking the mirror, "Who was I in a past life?" frame a question around a relationship, a skill, a phobia, or something that will help you understand your present life. "What was the first life that X and I were together?" "What was the life that brought forth my talent for_____?"

You can make the mirror part of a past-life regression with a hypnotist or past-life therapist. Having a facilitator will help keep you on track—they can pose questions and guide you along—and also help you deal with rushes of emotion, and for finding the high notes in whatever you experience. Some lives are pleasant and some are unhappy. Regardless, there is always something positive to glean from the experience.

In one of my workshops, a woman discovered a past-life in which she had been a man who was a bit of a scoundrel. This was upsetting to her, to think that she had been mean and dishonorable in another lifetime. There is always a thread to follow into the present that has healing and illuminating power. I asked her to see if there was someone in her present circumstances to whom she felt owed a debt, for there might be a rebalancing occurring now.

This past life could also serve as a "never again" reminder when certain circumstances arise. Past-life scrying might need to be augmented with other kinds of past-life recall work.

Remember that the mirror presents what you need, and when you explore in Truth you are given many opportunities for growth, healing and enlightenment.

Visiting the Akashic Records

The Akashic Records, the repository of everything in creation, are based on the concept of the *akasha* in Eastern mysticism and occultism. The *akasha*, a word derived from the Sanskrit term for "sky," is the all-pervasive life principle or all-pervasive space of the cosmos. It is the substance ether and the subtlest of all elements. It permeates everything in the universe and is the vehicle for all life and sound. In yoga, the akasha is one of three universal principles along with *prana*, the universal life force, and creative mind. These three principles are immanent in all things throughout the universe, and are the sources of magical and psychic power.

The concept of the *akasha* was introduced to Western occultism in the early twentieth century by Helena P. Blavatsky, founder of the Theosophical Society. As noted earlier, Blavatsky said the *akasha* forms the *Anima Mundi*, the "World Soul," and constitutes the soul and astral spirit of humanity. It produces mesmeric, magnetic and psychic phenomena, and is a component in all magical operations of nature. Blavatsky compared the *akasha* to the "sidereal light" of Rosicrucianism, the astral light of Eliphas Levi, and the odyle or odic force of Karl von Reichenbach. It is the equivalent of the Hebrew *ruah*, the wind, breath, air in motion, or moving spirit, and is identical with the spirit of God moving on the face of the waters. The akasha creates everything and keeps everything in balance—it is the "all in all."

Everything that ever happens throughout the universe—every thought, sound, emotion, action and so forth—is recorded permanently upon the *akasha*. The Akashic Records exist as impressions in the astral plane, and can be accessed by magical means, through clairvoyance (remote viewing) and by astral travel. The Akashic Records are consulted for information about past lives, lost civilizations and other planes of existence.

Spiritual beings such as angels provide assistance in accessing the records. The American trance psychic Edgar Cayce frequently consulted the Akashic Records to obtain past-life information that explained a client's health, personal and marital problems. Cayce said the astral repository was like a great temple filled with books.

Going to the Akashic Records, the cosmic archives of everything that ever was, is and will be, is often described as similar to visiting a vast library. Many people see the records as housed in a crystal temple, tended by guides who come forward to help you find what you are looking for. I see the records housed in a great temple of light. The temple is vast, beyond comprehension. It is filled with documents, sound recordings, collections of memories and thoughts, and pools of information that are difficult to describe, but which make themselves available in "direct knowing" ways. Information is accessed in a variety of other ways as well. You can hold a document and receive the pertinent information intuitively, or as a mental impression. You can review events and intentions. You can read, just like you would read a book now.

When I have gone to the Akashic Records, I see information contained in volumes like books, probably because I am a writer, and when I do my research, I read books and visit libraries. Others might go to film repositories or sound recordings. When I look at the book, I "get" information via mental impressions.

When you visit the Akashic Records, a guide will escort you to what you need to know, no more. Remember the guide, for he or she will help you again—a personal cosmic librarian.

Mirrors and dreams

Use the mirror to enhance dream incubation, which is the programming of dreams to answer a specific question. Dream incubation has been used since ancient times. The ancients often used dream incubation for healing, undertaking pilgrimages to remote locations for elaborate rituals. Others used dream incubation for contacting the dead. Today, dream incubation can be used for guidance, decision-making, divination, and contact with the dead and spirits. Phrase a single question. Enter the mirror for answers. End the session with the instruction to yourself that further information will be revealed in dreams, and you will remember them upon awakening. Note down your results from the scrying.

When you awaken, record everything you can remember about your dreams, even fragments, regardless of whether or not they seem to address the question. When you can, spend time analyzing the dream material, and see how it fits with your scrying session.

Mirrors and Tarot

Augment the mirror with insights from the Tarot. Frame a question, shuffle the Tarot deck, and set the cards aside. Enter the mirror and ask for answers to the question. After the close, draw a card from the deck. What additional information or perspective is revealed by the card? You can also do complete Tarot spreads to amplify the scrying.

Mirror readings

Give readings for others by scrying in the mirror. Ask the mirror to answer the other person's questions. Give the impressions as they come. Sometimes you will know the meaning of them, which you can interpret for the client. Other times, the images, impressions and symbols will make sense to the client but may not be clear to you. At the close, process all of the information for the other person. Give your intuitive interpretation.

Partnership scrying

Work with a partner in sessions. It's fun and also illuminating to see how your results compare. Try the technique of the magnetists. One person sits in front of the mirror and scries, while the other stands behind and focuses on the seated person's back of the head. Both of you will get impressions, in the mirror and mentally. According to occult principle, your magnetism energy will help manifest visions in the mirror for the other person. Trade off.

In another type of exercise, both of you sit in front of the mirror and scry, making private notes of what you experience. Compare notes at the close.

Remote viewing

Remote viewing trials are a great way to check and improve accuracy. You can do some of these exercises solo and some with a partner. "Remote viewing" is a modern term for clairvoyance, or "clear seeing" at a distance. It actually was coined for military applications, and makes use of geographic coordinates to identify the remote sites. It has come into general usage, however, and many people use it as a synonym for clairvoyance.

The very act of scrying is remote viewing, for the mirror or other shiny surface becomes the lens that peers into distant locations and penetrates time. When we visit the astral plane and the bridge to the afterlife, or look into past lives, we must analyze impressions on their face value. With structured remote viewing exercises of places and people in the physical world, you can check precisely how accurate you are.

You can remote view anything, as long as you have a way of checking accuracy later. It should not be a place or an object too familiar to you, or you might conjure up only what you know from memory.

A location might be a place you have never visited, which you ask to see in the mirror in as much detail as possible. Check against existing descriptions and photos. Even if you have a good idea of what the place looks like, there will be details unknown to you until they are revealed in the mirror.

You can also remote view future news events. How do you get the news every day? Internet, newspaper, television? Remote view the news source for the next day, or another future time. See and/or hear the news. Then check how accurate you are. Variations of this exercise, called book tests and newspaper tests, were devised in psychical research to test the powers of mediums. Some of the tests were quite complicated, such as remote viewing a certain line on a certain page in a book, or seeing a headline on a certain page of a future newspaper.

Try working with a partner. Have your friend move objects or furniture around in their home, keeping the rooms and moved items secret. Remote view and validate.

Have your friend place an object inside a box and seal it, and leave it out somewhere in their home. Find the box in the right room and remote view the contents inside. In a variation, have a friend write a message on a piece of paper and seal it in an envelope. Working remotely with the mirror, find the envelope and read the message inside.

How do you know if you remote viewed successfully or picked up thoughts telepathically from your friend? It is virtually impossible to draw clear lines (which has sent psychical researchers round in circles), but for these purposes it ultimately doesn't matter. In scrying work, psychic impressions come from a variety of sources and blend together, and these exercises are intended to increase your ability to receive them as accurately as possible. You can always try making a test more complex, such as a double blind.

By the way, for some peculiar reason, remote viewing and clairvoyance do not work well when it comes to predicting winning lottery numbers, or gambling wins. There have been limited successes, and even some controlled studies done by parapsychologists that yielded intriguing results. I participated in a long-term psychical research project myself, organized in England with international participants. That project involved coordinated meditation to get, or remote view, winning lottery numbers. All the reported numbers were crunched according to algorithms, and then tickets were bought from a pool of money. We had some successes, even winning streaks, but never the "big one."

Gambling is not a good way to use the mirror, anyway—it defeats the spiritual purpose you set in the beginning.

12

The Moon Factor

In ancient times, scryers gazed into the still water of a lake or pond at night. Their powers were enhanced if the light of the moon—especially a full moon—fell upon the water.

How much attention should be given to the moon and its phases in scrying activities? The moon has always been connected to the realms of dreams, intuition, psychic faculties, the spirit world and the dead, so paying attention to the moon stands to enhance your work. How much depth and detail you want to go into is up to you.

According to ancient wisdom, the waxing moon maximizes and magnifies, and the waning moon minimizes and decreases. This general principal has governed philosophies about the cosmic organization; rules of thumb for organizing activities in life; folk lore about using the moon in divination and spells; rituals in ceremonial magic; and concepts of alchemy.

Big magic

The moon has been regarded as a source of big magic since the earliest recorded history. Though both sun and moon have been worshipped, and the sun has been recognized as the giver of life, more magic has been based on the moon. The ancients observed connections between the moon's changing of phases and the natural rhythms of the tides and nature. Thus, they believed that the moon regulated body fluids and all life cycles as well. If one magically harnessed the mysterious force of the moon, one could influence life, it was reasoned. The waning moon was a time of decrease and the waxing moon a time of increase. The full moon represented plenty and the new moon represented a dark, uncertain time.

These ideas emerged from observations of the change in lunar shape. The sun appeared the same every day and never failed to rise. The moon, on the other hand, grew larger and then smaller, and for three nights in every cycle vanished completely from the heavens. This apparent death of the moon was not permanent, however, for the moon always resurrected itself anew.

Early humankind also observed that the moon's rhythms governed the rhythms of all life cycles: the tides, the rain, fertility, women's menstrual cycles, and plant life. It represented "becoming" and "being." The moon established a unifying pattern for all living things, living and breathing in harmony, existing in an intricate and ineffable web of interconnectedness.

This magical power to regulate life was perceived as early as the Ice Age, long before the discovery of agriculture. The moon was considered a force or power until about 2600 BC, when it became personified as the Man in the Moon, who, in some beliefs, could incarnate on earth as a king. The Man in the Moon gave way to lunar gods and goddesses.

Early peoples believed that the moon made all things grow, and governed all life-giving moistures. Its changing phases were associated with the coming of rain, as well as with the torrents that produced floods. The moon's fertilizing power governed not only plants and animals, but human beings as well. It was believed that women who slept out beneath the rays of the moon would become impregnated by them. Thus, as early mankind developed cosmogonies and mythologies, their deities associated with water, fertility and fecundity were also associated with the moon.

With the discovery of agriculture and animal husbandry, the lunar cycle became a guide for the planting and harvesting of crops and the slaughtering of animals. The deities overseeing these activities had lunar associations. With the development of healing arts, deities ascribed healing functions also were associated with the moon, for the moon was perceived to govern all the moistures within the body as well as in the external world. Rituals to influence all these aspects of life were addressed to the moon, and to the moon's representatives in the form of gods and goddesses.

Pliny the Elder, the first-century Roman naturalist, emphasized the importance of the moon in his *Natural History*, a set of 37 volumes dealing with the nature of the physical universe, anthropology, zoology, botany, geography and mineralogy. According to Pliny, the moon was central to the rhythms of the earth. He called the moon "the star of our life," and said that she fills and empties all bodies, including the blood volume in man, with her waxing and waning.

Pliny gave guidelines for planting, cutting, harvesting and getting rid of things in accordance with lunar phases. He also included lunar-based cures for many maladies.

Pliny's work is among the earliest organized body of lunar magic lore. *Natural History* served as an important source for lunar magic that evolved over the centuries.

The moon and the dead

Because of the moon's apparent rebirth in the sky every month, the moon became, in many cosmogonies, the repository of souls after death. Plutarch, the first-century Greek essayist and biographer, conceived of a lunar way-station for the going and coming of souls. Human beings had two deaths, he said. One occurred on earth, the domain of Demeter, the goddess of fecundity, when the body was severed from the mind and soul and returned to dust. The soul and psyche then went to the moon, the domain of Persephone, the Queen of the Underworld, where a second death took place with the separation of the two. The soul returned to the substance of the moon, where it was able to retain the dreams and memories of the life that had been lived. The mind, meanwhile, went to the sun, where it was absorbed and then gave birth to a new soul. In rebirth, the process was reversed: the sun sent mind to the moon, where it was joined with soul, then traveled to earth to join body and be born anew.

Similarly, the ancient Indians conceived of a "path of souls" and a "path of gods." As described in the *Upanishads*, the path of most souls was to the moon, where they would rest and await reincarnation. Those who had freed themselves of the need to reincarnate took the path of gods to the sun, which was beyond becoming.

The moon and scrying

The moon's influence over the fluids of life gives it connections to the element of water, which governs intuition, dreams, emotions, and the subconscious. Many scryers feel it is best to scry under the waxing and full lunar phases, and especially on a Monday, the moon's day. However, scrying can be done at other times with a shift in perspective.

Approaches to the waning moon

With all respect to ancient wisdom, the schedules of modern life are not always easy to arrange. I've done plenty of scrying and other psychic work under the waning moon, and with positive results. I just shift my focus and emphasis.

The waning moon is a time of decrease and banishment which can be harnessed to eliminate obstacles and prevent unhelpful forces and presences from interfering. When I scry during the waning moon, I start a session by emphasizing the elimination of all obstacles, the banishment of unproductive thoughts and impressions, and the banishment of any unhelpful presences. The unwanted is kept out as a matter of course in all scrying sessions in the asking for protection, but during a waning moon I give it a special emphasis.

I've never had any qualms about working in a waning moon. If you do your spiritual homework on a daily basis, protection goes with you all the time.

Void of course

Some individuals in psychic work also pay attention to lunar void-of-course times. The void of course is the period that lasts from the moon's departure from one sign of the Zodiac to its entry into the next sign. In lore, this is a time of uncertainty. When the moon occupies a sign, it exerts a certain influence, but in transit between them has nothing to affect. And so, it seems, the moon doesn't quite know what to do.

As a result, life below on earth can turn topsy turvy. Decisions made during the void-of-course have unexpected results. Newly purchased objects break, are defective or are left unused.

Agreements made that seemed rock solid change at a later time. It's a time when crazy and odd things happen, behavior is erratic, objects are misplaced, mistakes are made and we lose our way. Those who are accident-prone may have a mishap. Travel is subject to delays, cancellations and accidents.

Astrologers differ as to how significant the void-of-course influence is, however, most at least advise caution during these times. If possible, it's best to stick to routine matters and projects already underway. Avoid launching new projects, signing contracts, making major decisions (especially financial ones) and traveling. Wait to consecrate and charge a mirror.

Void-of-course times happen roughly every two to two-and-a-half days. Some voids last only for a few minutes, but most last several hours, and some for a day or more. Keeping track of them requires a dedication to detail.

As in lunar phases, the requirements of daily life have to be woven in. People the world over have scryed for millennia with and without factoring in lunar influences. The best approach is to experiment to find your comfort level. It is helpful to be in tune with cosmic forces, if nothing more than to be aware of them, and alter your psychic navigation accordingly.

Afterword

Now that you've learned about the black mirror, its colorful and extensive history, and how it works, it is time to give it a try. As with all tools in psychic work, use the black mirror with care.

Keep in mind that any type of spirit communication can elicit strong emotions, including unresolved grief. You may want to work with a therapist, or consult with one periodically. No matter what your purpose is in gazing, it is important to stay grounded and balanced.

For best results, do not overuse the mirror. Everyone has different thresholds, so pace yourself. In the beginning, it is easy to become fascinated and to want to spend more and more time at gazing. Mirror work should enhance your spiritual experiences, not govern your life.

Also keep in mind that people vary in the manner and speed in which they attune to the mirror. Do not give up if you have no or few results at first, and remember to pay attention to other avenues of results, such as dreams and synchronicity.

Appendix A

How to Make a Black Scrying Mirror

Making your own mirror is fun, and makes the mirror uniquely yours, imbued with your own creative energy.

Decide on your raw materials. You can purchase frames and have plate glass cut to fit, or buy ready-made photo frames with glass. If you have glass cut to fit, you can choose the thickness. I have found that ready-made photo frames serve well, even though the glass is thinner.

There are a variety of black coatings that are effective: flat black latex paint, black glossy latex paint, black enamel, and black marine flat and glossy paint.

I have not gotten good results at all with spray painting any of the above. Spray paint runs easily. For best results, clean the glass with a lint-free cloth and let it dry. Lay the glass flat on packing paper or newspaper, and apply paint with a high-quality roller. You will need several coats of paint, two to three depending on the paint, and each coat must dry thoroughly before you apply the next. Enamel paint takes much longer to dry than latex.

Avoid bubbles caused by improperly dried paint, and bumps caused by dirt and grit. If you use a brush instead of a roller, guard against dried brush strokes. When you turn the glass over, you want to see a smooth reflective surface. Bubbles, dirt and brush strokes will interfere with impressions and may even cause false ones.

Work in as clean an environment as possible, preferably indoors. I do not recommend painting the mirror outdoors, as there is too much dust and debris flying about that can land on the glass while it is drying.

Always handle the glass from the edges. Avoid touching the painted surface–you don't want fingerprints, either.

The process is fairly simple, but it is time consuming, and it is not unusual for glass to be ruined by small imperfections. Go slowly, be patient, and put your intentions into the mirror.

Frames can be turned into unique objects or art with personalized decorations. When I select ready-made frames, I look for well-made, ornate frames that have an antique or old feel to them. Vintage frames that are distressed are appealing, too. I also buy plain wood frames that can be stained, painted and decorated easily. You can paint symbols, angel names and other decorations, and you can glue on mixed media items to make your mirror truly one of a kind.

Appendix B

The Portable Altar

A person's home is sanctuary—a place where we love, dream, create and regenerate. It is a place where angels visit and the presence of God makes itself known.

Within the home, it is important to have a sacred space: a special place to pray, meditate, and do psychic work. Daily spiritual practice in a place builds up positive energy that benefits the home, as well as helps personal growth and spiritual attunement.

An altar anchors a sacred space. Traditionally, an altar is an elevated place where religious ceremonies are conducted, and where offerings are made. In a home, an altar serves as a focal point for one's private worship and communion. It is decorated with religious and personal objects whose symbolic meanings help our connection to the divine and the spirit realms.

Altars can be erected anywhere, such as on small tables in bedrooms, spare rooms and living rooms. They are unique to each person. Not everyone, however, has room for a permanent altar, even a small one. The perfect solution is the portable altar, which can easily be set up and then put away. Portable altars are ideal for travel as well.

For your scrying mirror portable altar, acquire a storage box big enough for the mirror, a pair of candles in small holders and or/several flameless tea light candles, a small cloth such as a kerchief or linen napkin, and other items of personal significance.

I travel a great deal, and have created a small portable altar that fits into a jewelry roll. It is ideal for home, too, because it stores neatly in the mirror box.

A jewelry roll is the perfect storage bag. It has zippered compartments that protect fragile objects, and can be rolled into a compact size. Choose a medium or large bag. The altar itself is established with the kerchief or cloth napkin, kept folded in one of the compartments in the roll. Mine is a silk pocket square that I bought in Japan. It bears an old silkscreen painting of the river of life framed by plum blossom trees. I place my altar objects on the cloth.

My altar reflects both West and East spiritual traditions. I have representations of the four elements, which in turn symbolize the four directions of Earth, as well as the four archangels of the heavenly quarters: Michael, who rules discernment; Gabriel, who rules beginnings; Raphael, who rules healing; and Uriel, who rules Truth.

For the fire element and to illuminate scrying, I use flameless tea light candles. Place one behind the mirror and one on either side. (If you are using real candles at home, place one on each side of the mirror.) For the water element, I have a tea light holder, which can be found in the candle sections of most stores; It serves as a small dish. At home, with more storage space, a goblet or cup can be used. For the air element, I have small feathers. For the earth element, I have a clear quartz crystal. Arrange the elements around the mirror.

For cleansing with smoke, I have a small brass incense burner just big enough to hold a cone of incense. I carry two or three cones in the roll along with the burner and a packet of matches.

I carry a small vial of frankincense essential oil in the jewelry roll. Myrrh is also good for scrying. A drop can be put in the water. You might dab a bit on the center of your forehead for the third eye faculty. Essential oils are strong, so be sure to dilute and use sparingly to avoid burning your skin.

Other items in my portable altar include prayer cards, small figurines of angels and religious figures, medallions of my favorite saints, and small jewelry pieces that have spiritual and mythological significance.

Other possibilities for a portable altar are meditation beads, pressed and dried flowers, stones, shells, and any mementoes that have a special spiritual significance to you.

Appendix C

Testimonials

In consideration of privacy, the following testimonials sent to me list no names or identifying personal details.

Female, age 40

I asked to see my youngest sister, who died when she was five and I was ten. I saw an image of her in the mirror. She appeared grown up, but I knew it was her, even though she never got the chance to grow up in life. She told me that people keep changing and growing in heaven. I told her I was sorry we never got to grow up together. She said she was always with me and all I had to do was think of her. It is true what they say, the dead are right beside us, a blink of an eye away. We talked about some other things, personal and family stuff. I know I will see her again.

Female, age 31

My best friend died in a car accident three years ago. I think about her a lot, and wanted to see if I could contact her using the black mirror. I didn't know what to expect, in fact, I was kind of skeptical about it. I saw her and heard her voice, clear as anything. She said she was okay and I should not worry about her. I felt immensely better.

Female, age 57

My husband had a heart attack and died at work before he could make it to the hospital. I was in such shock I could not believe it, and it took me a long time to pull myself out of the depths of incredible grief. I never got to say good-bye, and I was even angry that he was taken from me so soon. I did the mirror... it was five years since he'd gone. I felt at that point that I could handle it if he came and talked to me. The mirror got very cloudy, like gray clouds moving fast across a sky when it's completely overcast. All of a sudden he was talking to me, I could hear him in my thoughts. I told him how much I loved him and still missed him. He said he loved me too and he was sorry he had to go, but it was all right, and everything would be all right for me and the kids and grandkids. When we were done it seemed like a huge weight was gone. I still miss him, but talking to him did ease the pain.

Male, age 44

Curious more than anything. Asked to see my uncle who passed last year. We were really close and he was my favorite relative, especially when I was a kid. His wife, who died several years ago before him, came through instead and told me they were both fine, but he could not come to talk to me himself. Not sure why but had the feeling that's just the way it worked. I was glad just the same. An interesting experience, would do it again.

Female, age 60

I bought my own mirror and nothing happened the first few times I used it. Then it was like a door opened and I started seeing and hearing things when I did a session. I think I just had to get used to it. I have had several contacts. I see the faces in the mirror and hear their voices.

Male, age 51

After my father passed away, I had a dream about him in which I felt I was really with him. It was so real I have never forgotten it, and I wondered if the mirror could bring him back like that. He did come through, not exactly like the dream, but I did feel it was really him.

Female, age 36

I wanted to see if I could contact my guardian angel. While I was staring into the mirror I suddenly felt surrounded by a beautiful energy, warm and very loving. I "knew" this was my angel. It was such an incredible feeling, I can hardly describe it.

Female, age 34

I didn't try to communicate with anyone who's dead, but I tried an experiment to see my own home. After thinking hard about home and what it looks like, and gazing into the mirror, an image flashed across. I'm not sure if it was actually in the mirror or it was in my mind, or maybe it was both, who knows. I could see the dog sleeping on her pillow in the living room, and it was like I "walked" into the kitchen where my husband was getting a beer. I was kind of surprised because it was too early for him to be home. When I got home I told him about it and asked if he had come home early. He said yes he had wrapped up work and decided to leave early. He was home at about the time I was looking into the mirror. He was as surprised by it all as I was.

Male, age 52

I wanted to see a past life. I have tried past-life regression and thought doing it with a mirror would be interesting. I asked to see a certain life that I had seen in a regression. After a while the mirror got blurry and then I started seeing scenes and bits and pieces of this other life. It was definitely not fantasy because I was not controlling anything according to expectations. I did get some explanations and answers to questions.

Male, age 40

I work as a medium and sometimes I use a black mirror in readings with clients. It is very good for reaching the dead. Sometimes I have the client look in the mirror too. Once both I and the client saw the same thing (her deceased mother) in the mirror at the same time. It was very validating for the client.

Female, age 29

I never did anything like this before, but a friend told me I should try it. Amazing!

Female, age 44

I have experimented with other kinds of spirit communication methods, and I have found that the black mirror provides some of the strongest connections. I get a variety of impressions – images, feelings, words. No two experiences are the same. I agree that the mirror shows what you need to see or know.

Appendix D

Mirror Lore and Legends

Here is a collection of a few folklore beliefs about mirrors. Many of them here deal with divining a future spouse, a question of great importance to young people throughout the ages.

Early Vanity

A child who has not yet talked should never be held up to a mirror, for this encourages vanity.

To See Your Future Spouse

At night under moonlight, go outdoors and back backward several feet with a mirror in your hand, or, if indoors, walk several feet backward with a candle in one hand and a mirror in the other. Say:

> Round and round, O stars so fair!
> Ye travel and search out everywhere,
> I pray you, sweet stars, now show to me
> This night who my future husband/wife shall be

To Divine When You Will Marry

At a full moon, go to a stream or any body of water and hold a silk square over the water with the moon behind you. The silk will cause several reflections of the moon to be cast on the water. The number of reflections is the number of months before you will marry.

To Behold Your Future Husband

To see the face of your future husband, sit before a mirror and eat an apple (a fruit with a long history of divining power). Then start brushing your hair. An image of your future husband will appear in the mirror looking over your shoulder.

To Get a Man to Fall in Love with You

On a Thursday, secure a jet black hen which has never laid an egg and bury it at a crossroads. In three days dig it up, sell it, and use the money to buy a mirror. Bury the mirror that evening in the same spot as the hen, invoking the goddess of love, Venus. Sleep on the spot for three nights and dig up the mirror. Whoever looks into it will fall in love with you.

To Arouse Passion in a Woman

Buy a small hand mirror at the first price asked (without haggling). Scrape some pitch off the back and write the name of your beloved three times in this space. Hold it in front of two copulating dogs and ask your beloved to look into the mirror. Then hide it for nine days at a place where she passes by frequently. After that, always carry the mirror on your person. The passion captured by the mirror, along with the link to your beloved, will excite sexual passion.

Improve Vision

To remedy weak eyes, gaze fixedly into a mirror periodically.

Mirrors and the Dearly Departed

Back in the days when deceased people were laid out in homes prior to burial, it was a common custom to cover all the mirrors in the home, or turn them over to have their back sides facing out. It was believed that the dead lingered near their bodies until burial, and if they caught a glimpse of their reflections, they might become confused and not leave.

X-Ray Vision

A mirror framed on three sides only will give a witch telescopic and x-ray vision in order to watch others, especially enemies, who are at a distance. The proper magical words must be spoken to get the mirrors to work in this way. These magical mirrors were reputedly in use in England and some were brought to colonial America.

Bad Luck
Breaking a mirror brings seven years of bad luck.

Vampires and Mirrors
The notion that vampires cast no reflections in mirrors dates to 1897 and is the creation of Bram Stoker, author of the greatest vampire novel of all time, *Dracula*. Stoker drew on folk beliefs about mirrors reflecting the body and soul of a person. The vampire had no soul, so therefore could not cast a reflection in a mirror. In *Dracula*, a mirror reveals the true identity of Count Dracula, when Professor Abraham Van Helsing tricks the count into looking into a mirror on the under lid of a cigar or cigarette box.

The gimmick worked for Stoker, for silvered mirrors were not everywhere in the Victorian world. Thus, a vampire like the Count could hide in plain sight within society and artfully avoid mirrors.

For the better part of the next century, vampire novels and films that followed in Stoker's wake faithfully followed the mirror myth, too. But time and change caught up with even the deathless ones, and today's fictional vampires have found ways around the reflection problem—otherwise, they would be outed every time they ventured out on a public street.

Bloody Mary

Bloody Mary is an urban legend with many variations. The story goes that a girl named Mary fell seriously ill and was pronounced dead. She was still alive but in a coma, however, and tragically, she was buried alive. She woke up in her coffin and could be heard screaming at night, but by the time the coffin was exhumed, she was genuinely dead. Her unhappy ghost can be summoned in a mirror at night by repeating her name, Bloody Mary, three to five times while turning around. Her horrible face will appear in the mirror and, the ghost will scare (or stab) the person to death.

Faustian Mirrors

Different accounts are given of the story of Faust, who sold his soul to the devil in exchange for riches, knowledge and sex. In the Hollenzwang chapbooks dating to the early seventeenth century, there are magical recipes of all sorts, including for scrying. The recipes are similar to many other magical formulae for making enchanted mirrors. The following descriptions omit lengthy spells:

For making an Erdspiegel or Bergenspiegel, a mirror that will reveal all the hidden treasures of the earth, buy a new mirror on a Friday, paying whatever cost is asked so that no evil spirit can harm the mirror. Go to a churchyard cemetery at midnight and bury the mirror in a man's grave at the head, and leave it for nine Fridays. Remove the mirror, go to a crossroads, lay it in the middle and summon three spirits according to whatever purpose you have. Leave the mirror at the crossroads for nine Fridays and then return the spirits into the mirror with a spell. Take the mirror to a church altar and leave it for three Sundays, taking care that no blessing for the dead should be spoken over it. Then engrave the back side of the mirror with certain magical symbols. The mirror will then reveal hidden treasure and how to get it. For a magical divination mirror, get a round piece of iron and polish it, and get a second round piece of unpolished iron, and lay it over the top of the first piece. Lay a piece of wood or paper on top of both of them and smoke with incense. Then cut the wood or paper so that the polished iron can be framed by it and write the Tetragrammaton (sacred name of God) and other magical names on the frame. Recite certain magical names, and then use the mirror.

About the Author

Rosemary Ellen Guiley is a leading expert in the paranormal, metaphysical, and spiritual fields, and is the author of more than 50 books on spirit communications, paranormal investigation, dreams, intuitive and psychic development, entity contact experiences, angels and other subjects. She conducts workshops on black mirror scrying, dreamwork, psychic development and other topics. She is a former board member of the International Association for the Study of Dreams. Rosemary is a frequent guest on *Coast to Coast AM* and many other radio shows Her website is www.visionaryliving.com.

Bibliography

"A Mirror belonging to the Lady of Uruk." In *The Tablet and The Scroll: Near Eastern Studies in Honor of William W Hallo*, edited by Mark E. Cohen, Daniel C. Snell, David B. Weisberg, pp. 163-69. Bethesda, Maryland: CDL Press, 1993.

Atkinson, William Walter. *Practical Psychomancy and Crystal Gazing*. Yoga Publication Society, 1908.

Besterman, Theodore. *Crystal-Gazing*. New Hyde Park, NY: University Books, 1965.

De Laurence, L.W. *Crystal Gazing & Spiritual Clairvoyance.*
        Chicago: De Laurence, Scott & Co., 1913.

Dee, John. *A True and Faith Relation of What Passed for Many
        Years Between Dr. John Dee [...] and Some Spirits.* Preface
        by Meric Causabon. New York: Magickal Childe, 1992.
        First published 1659.

Guiley, Rosemary Ellen. *Dream Messages from the Afterlife.* New
        Milford, CT: Visionary Living, Inc., 2013.

_____. *The Encyclopedia of Magic and Alchemy.* New
        York: Facts On File, 2008.

Leitch, Aaron. *The Angelical Language Volume I: The Complete
        History and Mythos of the Tongue of Angels.* Woodbury,
        MN: Llewellyn Publications, 2010.

Melville, John. *Crystal-Gazing and the Wonders of Clairvoyance.*
        London: Nichols & co., 1903.

Moody, Raymond with Paul Perry. *Reunions: Visionary Encounters
        with Departed Loved Ones.* New York: Villard, Books,
1993.

Northcote, Thomas W. *Crystal-Gazing.* London: Alexander Loring
        Ltd., 1905.

Printed in Great Britain
by Amazon